Pres

MW01440963

Thought This one
May be of interest —

Books By Helen Powers

Signs of Silence, 1972

The Biggest Little Cat Book in th World, 1978

A Parent's Guide to the 5 U.S. Military Academies, 1986

The Biggest Little Cat Book in the World, 1989

Stories of Our People, 1995

Winding Roads

A New England Notebook of Wisdom and Wit

By

Helen Powers

1999

Limited Editions
P.O. Box 572
Rocky Hill, CT 06067

Copyright © 1999 by Helen Powers

All rights reserved. No part of this book may be reproduced, stored in a retrieval system, or transmitted in any form or by any means, electronic, mechanical, photocopying, recording, or otherwise, without the permission of the author..

ISBN: 0-7392-0164-6

Library of Congress Catalog Card Number: 99-94258

Printed in the United States of America by
Morris Publishing
3212 E. Hwy. 30
Kearney, NE 68847
1-800-650-7888

Gracias

To Ellen and Bill Burnett at the New Fairfield *Citizen News* where these columns first appeared, and to all my wonderful readers around Candlewood Lake; the Pyquag Writers, Ellie, Maryanne, Maria and Susan, who were tough editors; Phyllis Sanderson, Jane Seraphin, Janice Hurley, Joan Polteraitis, and Judy Sartucci, friends who were always ready for anything; my family, Larry, Lorrie and my son Tim for putting up with me; my grandchildren Katie and Mike whose every visit gave me new material for another column; my agent Jim Cypher who taught me where to use commas (among other things); and, last but best, K.M.K., without whom . . . . . yadda yadda yadda.

CONTENTS

INTRODUCTION   1

JANUARY   5
    Country Living - The Dark Ages - Little House on the Prairie - Time to Take Inventory - The Heartbeat of January

FEBRUARY   17
    New England Winter - Winter in Wisconsin - School's Out! - Moon Over Miami - Queen Elizabeth Cure - Homebodies - Condo Comfort

MARCH   29
    Tea for Two - Grandfather's Clock - Seed Catalogues - Modern Inconveniences Neptune's Children - Speed - Winter is Over

APRIL   41
    Laughter - Condo Cats - Living off the Land - Dinner in the Diner - Eaater Bonnet - The Dining Room Drawer - Plant a Tree - Midas I'm Not

MAY   57
    Late Spring, Early Summer - Breezes Blow - Lost in the Bronx, Found in Queens - Rhubarb - Utopia - Breaking Holiday Traditions - Decoration Day - Rewriting Our Lives

JUNE   69

World Traveler - Housewife - The River Says "Slow Down" - Bon Appetit! - Summer Heat - Country Evenings

JULY   83

Picnic in the Park - Hats Off to the Fourth of July - Miracles - Heat Wave - Bar Harbor - Electronic Demons - Solitude

AUGUST   97

Queen Anne's Lace - The Meadows of Our Minds - Pretty is as Pretty Does - Zucchini Attack - V-J Day - Dead Bird - Cicada Serenade - Summer's Treasures

SEPTEMBER   113

Fallen Leaves - Tag Sale Tillie - Early Retirement - Toys in the Attic and Every Place Else - Bubbie, I Love You - Room With a View - L'Chaim!

OCTOBER   126

Day Trips - The Beach in October - Pitiful Pets - Living Clean is the Best Revenge - Housemates I Have Known - North Wind Blows

NOVEMBER   143

The First Snowflake - The Hall Closet - Trendy Foods - The Palatinates - Thanksgiving - The Ultimate Revenge - The First Snowfall

DECEMBER   159

Rock Church Novena - Preparing for Winter - The Great Aunts - City Christmas - The Empty Next -Caroling on Christmas Eve - Noel - Searching for an Earlier Day

Introduction

Like many women in mid-life, when I became a widow, I found myself living alone in a house that was too big for me and too expensive to maintain. The children were grown and gone, and my husband had been put to his final rest in the hallowed grounds of the Catholic cemetery nearby. I clanked around like Ceasar's ghost while I debated whether or not I was ready to toss in the sponge and give up the house that had given us so much pleasure as a family. It's not an easy decision to make. Memories are more binding than chains; tradition dies hard.

The four-bedroom house sat high on a hill overlooking a lake. It was a house for all seasons. Surrounded by woods, we had the added bonus of nature. Woodchucks, chipmunks, rabbits, squirrels, possum and deer abounded on our land. Cardinals, finches and blue jays ate at our feeders, and birds of every description could be seen on the branches of the trees near the house. I wanted for nothing, but there was too much of everything.

We had raised both boys in the house. For the nine years our younger son was in the Navy, it was his harbor, the place he returned to from all over the world. To my grandchildren it was "Grandma's house," where the family gathered for holidays and

Winding Roads

family celebrations. Obviously there was more to consider than myself.

Finally, when my son and his family moved to the other end of the state, I put the house on the market. I began looking at condos closer to where they had moved. My search ended when I found a spacious condominium with an attached garage, a first floor bedroom, a formal dining room, central air, and two master bedrooms with private baths. Outside there were rolling green lawns, woods and views. It offered all the joys of country living without the work.

Once I found the condo I wanted, it became an obsession. Every week I drove up and went through the display house. I saw myself living in it. I dreamed about the life I would find there. It was both agonizing and inspiring. It held me together in those years following the death of my husband, because I was looking ahead, preparing myself for a change. This was the dream that kept me going.

When my real estate agent told me we had a serious offer on the house, I selected my unit from the four that were left and put down a binder. Another dream had come true. It is said that if we live as though we are what we want to become, or as though we have what we want to acquire, it becomes a reality. I saw myself living in the condo for two years before I moved there.

Any sadness over leaving the house was wiped away by my excitement over my new condo. I wasn't giving up anything; I was making a carefully considered move to better accomodate the changes that had taken place in my life.

The timing was right. I did not want to be at the other end of the state in my "declining" years, as I felt that would be too hard on my children. They would worry about me and feel obligated to visit to make certain I was all right. In the event of my illness, their burden would be even greater because of the distance. I went through this with my own parents, and I knew how hard it was. Also, I didn't want to be removed from the house arbitrarily when I was no longer able to handle the move myself. I wanted to relocate while I was still in a position to make new friends and become familiar with my surroundings.

I would have a chance to help with my grandchildren when the need required. I would be a blessing, not a burden. I could see my children often, but for shorter periods of time. This is much better than an all-day siege that is necessary when the drive takes a couple of hours. It's easier on everyone.

When we locked the door of the house for the last time, I didn't look back. I looked forward. I had done what I had to do. The day I closed on the condo and walked through its empty rooms, I knew that the winding road had led me home.

Winding Roads

Chapter

1

January

January 2

When I bought my condo, I made up my mind that it would become my "little place in the country." I had read all the magazine articles describing the abstract joys of "country living," but, having spent my own childhood summers on my grandfather's farm in Missouri, I knew what "country" was all about. I knew that it wasn't about the clutter and collections pictured on the slick pages of the magazines where the furniture is so close together no one could walk between the chairs. The country I would strive for would be the pure country of my childhood. There would be no milk glass collections on my shelves and no rusty kitchen utensils hanging from the ceiling.

I would create a country atmosphere that would ameliorate the stress of daily living. It would have to be more

Winding Roads

than ruffles and folk art. The "country" I remember from childhood was a way of life, not just a decor. My grandfather's farmhouse in Missouri was a place to come back to after long hours in the fields, where the warmth of a woodstove and the soft, golden glow of a kerosene lamp rewarded the toils of a hard day's work. I would avoid clutter and reach instead for an authentic simplicity that would allow the open space to breathe. This is what "country" means to me.

My condo came to life as soon as I settled in. The chintz and checks that predominate the decor are showcased against white walls.

I am the fourth generation in my family to use the heavily carved oak dining room furniture which is more than seventy-five years old. This is a departure from the country style I favor, but back in the thirties the farmhouse was furnished with whatever its owner happened to "come by." I "came by" my dining room set when my aunt moved into an apartment, and she "came by" it when her aunt died. I added a display cabinet for my mother's and grandmother's old cut glass and a tea cart I found in an antique shop.

The only thing "country" about my kitchen is the view. The contemporary room is compact, but more than adequate. Like the living room, it, too, is angled and has five walls, one of which is floor-to-ceiling glass. The view looks across the deck to a rolling lawn dotted with tall trees and bordered by a lightly wooded area, a pleasant reminder of the fields we used to gaze upon from the farmhouse windows in Missouri. Thanks to my glass-walled kitchen, I am in touch with nature and in tune with the rhythm of the seasons.

Back in the Midwest every farmhouse worth its salt had a

first floor bedroom, and this was high on my list of priorities. My first floor bedroom has an adjoining bath and is furnished with the bird's eye maple bedroom set my father bought for me when I was a child. At the foot of my bed is an antique chest I "came by" when a close friend of mine moved to Florida. It conceals a small television that I can watch from my favorite corner of the room.

However, the thing that really makes my bedroom "country" are the ragamuffin cats that sleep in the sun on my grandmother's handmade quilt. Nothing conveys the country ideal like a cat. It is impossible to disassociate the country from animals, because every farm had its faithful family dog and a constantly changing number of barnyard cats. I consider my shaggy dog and my cats to be an important part of my decor. They make a major contribution to the peace and fulfillment I find here.

Upstairs I have an over-sized guest room with lace-hung windows, and a private bath. In true country fashion, none of the furniture in the bedroom matches, but the casual blend brings to mind the big upstairs bedroom at my grandfather's farm. In many ways I have recreated a favorite part of my past.

My condo-house is cozy and snug. My studio is under the eaves. With a skylight overhead, it is bright and cheerful on the most dismal day when the wind swirls the snow outside in feathery eddies of ice. I feel like a rabbit inside a hollow log, braced against winter, waiting for spring.

Living alone seems far less lonely if we create a warm, friendly environment in our home. It should be a haven in the frenzy of activities that demand our time and attention on the outside, a place we look forward to coming back to. With a little imagination and a touch of color, the smallest apartment can be transformed into a "nest."

Closed inside our houses and cut off from neighbors and friends by drifting snow, we are almost as isolated as our forefathers were when they came here in the 17th century. The family unit gathers around a roaring fire, and experiences again the spirit of unity that was the spine of the early settlements in this country. Submerged in snow, our modern highways resemble the pioneer trails that lie beneath the asphalt and concrete we have there now.

January 13

A sigh of relief resounds when the holidays are over. We are stuffed and overstuffed with food. We have indulged our appetites until we are satiated. We yearn for light meals, fresh fruit and vegetables. It is time to return to a simpler diet. Our bodies know; if not, our mirrors tell us. We have visited with friends, entertained our families, and partied every weekend since Thanksgiving. We're ready for winter. If a party is canceled by bad weather, it's a gift of time we hadn't anticipated, and we are delighted. We need space to rekindle our lives.

Once the Christmas tree comes down and the glow of the colored lights is missing from the living room window, winter unleashes its glory in full spate. The Dark Ages will prevail for two more months, the only satisfaction being that each day is a minute or two longer than the day before.

We put on our heaviest clothing to ward off the seasonal chill in spite of our central heat and comparative comfort. A warm woolen sweater is never out of place in January. We bundle

Winding Roads

up even more to walk to the mail box, shoving our feet into boots, and pulling a knit hat down over our ears while we swaddle our faces in scarves and mufflers. By the time we get back, we know we've been there.

Winter foods are the most nourishing, as they supply the body with much needed heat. We stop buying green canteloupe shipped in from California and eat citrus fruit instead, sweet pink grapefruit and oranges from Florida. Homemade soups and stews are the order of the day. Homemade bread makes them even better. Freshly popped corn is also a treat whether it is made over the open fire or in the microwave. The fragrance alone warms the body and comforts the child in all of us.

The isolation that a blizzard inflicts is especially good for our souls. Our bodies may complain about lack of exercise, but our souls rejoice in the solitude. In this day and age, we seldom have time to think. We have become so riddled with noise and activity that we must relearn the art of being alone with ourselves and indulging in the kind of contemplation that the great thinkers thrived on centuries ago. Solitude provides a revival of the spirit. Great thoughts are frequently shunted aside by our normal lives, our jobs, and our duties. Now is the time to balance the books.

Winter gives us a chance to get in touch with ourselves and each other. It is nature's reprieve. Although man does not need the deep hibernation of a bear or a rabbit, he, too, needs this period of darkness and solitude to patch up the cracks in his foundation and sort out his thoughts that are scrambled by survival the rest of the year. We should rejoice in nature's plan and live the season to its fullest.

Winding Roads

January 15

Winter is a good time for reading, particularly in front of a roaring fire, snugly and warm as a kitten. Recently I bought a complete set of "Little House" books for my granddaughter. Since I had never read them myself, I decided to do this before I gave them to her. "Little House on the Prairie" was always one of my favorite series on television. I enjoyed the close-knit family warmth that developed from their isolation and the unsophisticated pleasures that filled their waking hours. I was envious of the simplicity of the family's lifestyle.

Laura Ingalls Wilder's personal account of life on the prairie and the frontier revealed a different story from that which was shown on television. It was a hard life. Most of their energy went into survival. She tells about long, stormy winters when they lived on nothing but turnips and potatoes. Butter was a luxury that rarely graced their table. The blizzards and storms that battered the Midwestern plains were challenging. The roughly hewn cabins in which they lived could not keep out the cold, and the small wood stove that was their heat source did not warm the room. The windows were solidly iced most of the winter. In order to draw warmth from each other, the little girls slept two to a bed like puppies.

On the prairie frontier Christmas meant a couple of pieces of hard candy and possibly a small homemade toy. Everything was homemade, and whenever the girls' fingers thawed enough to handle a needle, they sat working on knit laces, knit stockings, and embroidery. Laura's mother made all their clothes without a sewing machine, and her father built their cabins in a couple of days, then made the crude furniture that went inside of them. We didn't see these hardships on television.

In spite of all this, they became as excited over a bouquet

of wildflowers as I would over a new Benz. The appearance of meat on the table in winter, whether it was a rabbit or a venison steak, brought about a party mood because it meant they would have gravy to put on their potatoes and dry bread. The things we can't live without, they never dreamed of acquiring.

It is amazing that the Ingalls could survive the long, cold winter on a diet of starch alone. Both the potatoes and the turnips were the fruits of their own labors. These were the vegetables that would keep all winter. Orange juice was unheard of, so their overall vitamin deficiency must have been acute. Nevertheless, they survived, and Laura even prospered.

This was true "country living" a century or so ago, but I have no desire to go back that far after reading these books. It is difficult to understand why a man would choose such a hard life for himself and his family. I never thought about the realities of their day-to-day living, such as where their food, clothes and shelter came from, nor was I aware of how hard they had to work. My country condo will never be the little house on the prairie. I'd freeze to death.

January 20

The in-house days of January offer an opportunity to take inventory, not of our worldly goods, but of our spiritual and emotional possessions. We reassess our lives, re-establish our goals, re-assert our good intentions, and trim the budget. It puts us in touch with ourselves and makes us more aware of those things that are important to us. Then, as the weather changes, we quickly revert to old habits and go merrily on our way.

Winding Roads

Some industrious people do their spring housecleaning in mid-winter, so they will not be confined indoors when the weather turns. They go through closets and drawers, paring down to make room for more purchases and things that will have to be pared down later. This is a very sound idea, and I like it, but it never works for me. I enjoy the winterscape as much as that of summer or spring, so my head and eye keep wandering back to the outdoors while my body keeps warm inside.

This is also an excellent time to do a little redecorating to give the house the lift it seems to need this time of year. What better time to paint or paper or add new slipcovers or pillows? I keep a packing box of curtains in the closet, and when I get the urge for a change, I switch the curtains in a room. Most of my windows get a "new" look in January. The box also contains bedspreads and pillows so that, if I like, I can change the entire color scheme of one of the bedrooms. This saves me the expense of going out and buying new, and I never fail to be surprised by the forgotten treasures I find in my box.

A few of my friends turn to the kitchen in winter. They bake their own bread and turn out any number of items for the freezer, from entrees to desserts. I am not this dedicated to the stove, but I like a pot of homemade soup, brown beef broth with barley and onions, or a savory, steamy stew when the snow is on the ground. My favorite wintertime dessert is old-fashioned bread pudding, a gentle reminder of days gone by. Hardly anyone makes bread pudding any more, but it can be found on my table once every week or two when the weather is cold and the temperature outside falls below freezing.

January can be a productive month. It is a great time to learn something new. Several years ago when I first became

Winding Roads

conscious of the irreversible ticking of my body clock, I made up my mind that I would learn something new every year. The challenge is stimulating and the accomplishment, rewarding. The first year of my "enrichment" program, I bought a word-processing electronic typewriter and learned how to use it. The next year I studied photography. I became adept enough to do my own photos for stories and books. The year after that I bought my first computer without having the vaguest idea what a computer was. Self-taught, I have spent nine years since then grasping the intricacies and the unlimited possibilities of these amazing machines.

Another year I began playing the organ, something I had wanted to do all my life. Last year I took up sketching, and this year I have a new computer system that could occupy me for the rest of my life. I sit here by the hour exploring ways and means of accomplishing tasks that I used to do by hand. The discipline of learning is helpful in all areas of our lives and should never be abandoned.

Another skill I added to my repertoire last year was genealogical research. We are fortunate to have a Latter Day Saints (Mormon) library nearby. I learned to use their files and spent hours in the pursuit of my ancestors. It's like putting together a giant jigsaw puzzle, carrying with it the same excitement when we find a piece that fits. I didn't realize what I was getting into when I started. The spelling of family names changes frequently, and three generations back the male members of the family married two or three times. As one wife died, the widowed husband took another. In addition to this, it is almost impossible to find reliable records prior to 1850. The task became so mind-boggling I put it aside until my son gave me a genealogy program for my computer, so I am off and running again.

Winding Roads

January 31

January is the time to enjoy the spectacular beauty of a winter storm. At this time of year a wintry blizzard rolls through Connecticut every three or four days, bringing with it a variety of traffic-snarling conditions that range from freezing rain to heavy snow. The snow steals quietly over the land with a sugar-frosting sweetness while the white night lies silent and sleeping. The next day freezing rain turns the trees into spun-glass fantasies that glisten and glow in the morning sun. We are privileged to find such breathtaking splendor on our landscape, turning every window into a frame for a fleeting view of nature's art.

Of course, for people who have to trudge into the office over slick roads and freshly fallen snow, January is treacherous and tedious, but for those who can stay inside, it is a period of contentment and hibernation.

The heartbbeat of January is best felt on a day when the falling snow is swirled from the rooftops by a northwest wind that signals temperatures dropping to zero. It is a beautiful time to be indoors, snug as a squirrel with a year's supply of nuts. I go out only if I have to. There is a coziness in my condo that I was never able to achieve in the house. It was too big. Here the rooms wrap around me like a cocoon, and I am safely sealed inside.

Winter in Connecticut doesn't seem to be what it was twenty or even ten years ago. This is not "old-timer" talk; this is true. When we arrived here from the Midwest, the snow fell in December and stayed on the ground until March. Blizzards and drifts frequently left us housebound for two or three days. Every winter was an adventure. The pantry was well stocked in anticipation of the storms, while candles and kerosene lamps stood in readiness. Left without power, we listened to the

Winding Roads

portable radio and played games in front of the fire. It was a time of peace and togetherness.

Winters are milder now, or maybe they seem that way because I have left the northwest hills and moved back into town. When I lived in the country, each visit from the snow plow was followed by a bill. Now that I am living in a condo, the snow plow is part of our service, and the men who clear our street and driveways also sweep and scrape our front steps.

My house on the hill became inaccessible when the snow fell. Until we had a good thaw, I couldn't get down to the road for the mail or the paper. Now my paper is at the front door, and the mail box is just across the street. We are never snowed in. The roads are flat, and we can always get to the store. There is no denying that the scenery and the challenge were greater in the country, but I have come to enjoy the urban conveniences that city living offers. It takes the edge off of winter.

As January comes to an end, the darkest days of winter are behind us. I rejoice in the soft silence of a house that is quiet, but not lonely. I rejoice in good health and good cheer because I am happy where I am. I turn off the lights and say goodnight to January. Then I tuck myself into a warm bed, and fall asleep in the feathery softness of childhood dreams.

Winding Roads

Chapter 2

February

February 2

February arrived this year like a breath of spring. This is unusual. It is normally a blustery, bitter cold month, but we were teased by April-like weather when we turned the page of the calendar. With temperatures hovering around 60 degrees, I stretched out on the deck to enjoy the warmth of the sun one afternoon and walked the trails in a nearby park on the next. In the shaded lowlands where I hiked, bogs were ice-covered, and the chill of winter could still be felt. Then the weather changed, and we found ourselves back where we should have been in the first place.

The snowbirds have gone south for the winter. Only the hardy remain in their homes. We enjoy complaining about the weather, and we are gladdened beyond belief by one bright, sunny day. We thrive on the contrasts of the New England winter.

Winding Roads

February 10

When we were on the corporate trail, we lived briefly in Wisconsin. With the exception of International Falls and possibly Siberia, it must have been one of the coldest places on earth. All winter we could not go outside without wrapping our faces in scarves because the air was too cold to make contact with our lungs. Even then, our nostrils iced the minute the door closed behind us.

We moved one day in January when the temperature never climbed above 29 degrees below zero. Our clothes froze to our bodies and stuck there. On any given day in mid-winter, we were delighted if the temperature reached zero.

When I dressed my five-year-old to walk the half block across an open field to the schoolhouse, he had on so many layers of clothing he couldn't lower his arms. He moved like a snowman, but it was an adventure. The cold never kept him indoors.

We went to cocktail parties in high-necked woolen dresses with Damart underneath. For formal affairs we put on floor-length wool skirts with turtlenecks and blazers. The stockings we wore were so thick we didn't have to shave our legs all winter. We didn't shed our heavy coats until May. By comparison, I am in the tropics now.

February 17

February means winter vacation in most of the schools. Like grandmothers across the country, I found myself with a seven-year-old house guest for the week. She's adorable, and I love her, but she is perpetual motion and non-stop babble. By Wednesday I understood why only the young have babies.

In the course of the week, we went to the library, attended a Teddy Bear Picnic, visited the park, drove down to the shore and went shopping. Friday night her three-year-old brother joined the party. I put them to bed at 8:00, again at 8:15 and again at 8:30. This went on until almost 11:00.

They were up bright and early the next morning. With the temperature standing at thirteen degrees, Michael insisted on going outside to blow bubbles. I told him it was too cold, but he started screaming, so I helped him into his coat. He put up a good fight when he had to come in, and once inside, he refused to take off his hat and jacket.

Katie, in the meantime, had put on one of the new outfits we had bought for her on Thursday, harem pants with a short-sleeved cotton top. I told her it was not warm enough for short sleeves, but she began to cry, so I said, "Wear it!" Discipline was down the tubes.

Pooped to the point of no return, I remembered a pleasure from my own childhood and suggested they build a giant maze in the guest room. I gave them an old bedspread, several pillows, and a blanket. It was quiet for almost a half an hour while they diligently tipped over furniture and covered it with quilts.

When I fixed their lunches, they wanted to eat in the maze. At this point I didn't care if they ate on the roof of my car. They took their lunches upstairs, but while they were washing their hands, the dog went into the maze, and ate the sandwiches. When they came down to get the new meals I had fixed for them, Michael's foot went into the cats' water bowl, spilling its contents across the kitchen floor.

At 1:30 they were picked up by their other grandparents,

and not a moment too soon. I kissed them good-bye and said I would see them some time in August, although they only live ten minutes from my house.

I couldn't face the maze in the guest room, the water on the floor, or the bubbles that had frozen in the container on the deck, so I got into the car and drove away. The pain in my back and the aching exhaustion began to leave my body as I reached the highway, and by the time I returned home, I felt great, so I cleaned the house, changed the beds, and did laundry. I was reminded again of how much of our exhaustion is psychological. No one gets tired when they're having fun.

February 22

Once that was over, my friend Phyllis and I decided to drive to Florida for a brief reprieve from our daily duties. Since neither of us are great travelers, it was a history-making event, mainly because we actually arrived at our destination.

Our first surprise came when we reached Charleston, South Carolina, without turning around to go home. This we did in less than two days. When we stopped in Charleston, everything was in blossom and bloom, a breathtaking sight in February. We spent a day there visiting some of the nearby plantations and walking along the Battery. The Southern architecture of the city, row houses the color of the spring flowers they sell on the streets, and the heady scent of oleander and hyacinths fulfilled all our dreams of what the South should be.

It's not hard to imagine the past grandeur of this beautiful antebellum city. Walking next to the water and looking at the fine

Winding Roads

old homes that line the street, it is easy to slip into the pages of history of one of the South's most picturesque cities. We could almost hear the music playing as Southern ladies danced beneath the stars in their gossamer gowns and hoop skirts. Then the War began, and everything changed. The Union victory reunited the country, but to this day there is an unspoken separation between North and South.

We reluctantly left this leisurely lifestyle and pursued our trek with diligence. By the time we finally reached our friends in Delray Beach, we had been gone five days. We received a warm welcome 'midst picture postcard beauty.

Florida never seems real to me. I think someone made it up. The sunshine and the palm trees create a tropical ambience that brings out the Gaugin in all of us. It's another world, a tradewind paradise, marred only by bugs the size of baseballs.

Our friends live in a beautiful home on the water with manicured lawns and flowering shrubs. The floors in the house are marble. From the lanai we could hear the wash of water on the sandy beach a few feet away. Coming from New England where everything is cozy, cuddly and warm, we felt it was an abstract way of life. There is a temporary feeling in Florida, quite contrary to the continuity and permanence we find in Connecticut.

Certainly the sunshine and the palm trees are particularly welcome in this, the most dismal month of the year. We managed to see a couple of our friends between their bridge games and golf, people who have taken up year-round residence in the Sunshine State. Everyone we met seemed to be happy there, but after a few days Phyllis and I were ready to get into the car and head back to the weary remains of winter that awaited us in New England.

The trip home never takes as long as the trip away. Maybe

Winding Roads

we drive faster because we're eager to get there. We enjoyed the visit and the mid-winter summer, but home was a welcome sight. How wonderful it is to come back to the comfort and familiarity of the place where we live. No matter how luxurious the vacation may be, home is always best.

February 25

Both George Washington and Abraham Lincoln were born in February. They were role models for their generation. Parents with high hopes named their sons for each of these men. Role models are an important influence on a child's growth, development, and goals.

One of my best role models which has served me well since childhood is Queen Elizabeth, not because she is the richest woman in the world, but because of the manner in which she conducts herself.

When Queen and I were little, we were the same age, although she's much older than I am now. I remember the Princess as a child. She would appear in her organdy ruffled dress, silk knee socks with rosettes on them, and black patent leather shoes. Whether she was playing with her dog in the park or riding her bicycle on a windy day, she never got dirty or mussed.

The Princess grew up to become the Queen of England. How many times have we seen this amazing woman standing on the balcony at Buckingham Palace waving to her subjects in a pouring rain, without getting wet?

She can attend a polo game in a windstorm with every

Winding Roads

hair in place. She can tour darkest Africa in tsetse fly season, but she never sweats. No matter what the situation or the weather, she is calm, cool and collected. She never coughs, sneezes or blows her nose in public. She can stand in a receiving line for two hours without changing the expression on her face or showing any signs of discomfort or fatigue. How, I often wonder, does one achieve this kind of poise and control?

Queen Elizabeth is human like the rest of us. She has endured childbirth, no doubt stoically, she gets headaches and head colds. Sometimes her feet hurt or her back aches, but if she is scheduled to open Parliament when a toothache hits, she carries on bravely and fulfills her duties in good spirits. She is dedicated to her responsibilities. She lives up to all expectations.

The only difference between Queen and the rest of us (outside of several billion dollars) is that she has been trained and disciplined to fulfill her obligation in life, which is basically that of a role model for all of England. She represents the monarchy and the women of her country in the best light, and this she does flawlessly. She grew up with this kind of discipline and responsibility.

Sixty years of diligent Queen-watching have given me a clue to improving my own self-control and poise. I call it the "Queen Elizabeth Cure." When I find myself in a "situation," whether it's a root canal or a lecture in front of 300 rowdy octogenarians in Jersey, I adopt the Queen's attitude and her posture. I say softly, "Queen Elizabeth." This conjures up an instant image of the Queen. My shoulders go back, and I stand straight as she would do. My hands fold in front of me, my heart rate slows, and I am in control. I am poised and at peace. I take a deep breath as I say "Queen Elizabeth" again to myself. I am ready for anything. I can stand in the rain without getting wet.

I had a number of other, more superficial, role models in my childhood, most of whom were movie stars. I curled my hair like Bette Davis; I tried to sing like Jeanette McDonald and wanted to skate like Sonja Henie. Although I never achieved my ultimate goals, I was better for having tried.

Once when we went to my grandfather's farm in midwinter and the pond in back of the house was frozen, I went out in the bitter cold to skate after dinner in the moonlight. I was exhilarated. For about fifteen minutes, until I lost the feeling in my feet, I glided across the rough ice, and the sound of the blades of my skates transported me to Norway. It was a golden experience. For a brief moment I achieved the status of my role model, a moment that never came again.

Our role models influence how we dress, how we act, and what we choose to do with our lives. The impressions they make upon a child are manifest in the adult. They establish our goals and give us something to strive for. Everything starts with a pattern or a plan, and our role models impart this to us with the lasting impressions they make.

It is important that we remember that we may be role models for someone else. When we were young, there was always an older cousin or big brother whom we wanted to imitate, and then one day we are that "older cousin" for someone else. What we do and how we act are important all our lives. If we can touch another's life and, through our example, help just one person to do whatever it is he or she does, better, then we have done a wonderful thing. We must carry on the tradition and become role models such as we once had ourselves.

Winding Roads

February 27

I no longer have a fireplace. Sometimes I miss it, but even without it, I find winter to be the very essence of New England living. Snow-covered villages nestled in the hills, marked by soaring steeples, dot the mythical landscape on Christmas cards, but for us who live here, the myth is real. Whether in Vermont, Connecticut or Maine, we are a part of the American scene as it has been pictured for centuries, and not much has changed since it all began.

Certainly the changing seasons are a treasure. We live in eager anticipation, always on the threshold of something "better." In February the calendar is nudging spring. The hardy New Englanders feel a sense of victory for having endured another winter. Life goes on; beauty abounds.

When the sleet is hitting my skylight like pebbles, I revel in the warmth of my house. I may spend more time at home or more time alone, but it's a grand opportunity to sort out my life, clean the hall closet, or work on a project that is invariably put aside when the weather is more condusive to going outdoors. I refocus my energy and appreciate what I have.

Only rarely does the weather keep us in when we have some place to go. We bundle up like Eskimos to attend the opera or the theater. We visit our favorite restaurants and eat in front of an open fire to the crackle and crunch of burning logs. After all, this is what New England is about. Winter is an acceptable part of our landscape.

My dog Phoebe and I are basically homebodies. We like the warmth and aroma of our kitchen, and we sleep best when we are tucked in our own bed under a warm comforter on a cold night. Every room in the house becomes a nest in winter, each with its own purpose to fulfill.

Phoebe is a bigger homebody than even I may be. When I put her into the car to go to the groomer or the vet, she is so distraught about being taken from her familiar surroundings that she cries and trembles all the way there. She is fine on the ride home. At least I'm not that bad, but, like Phoebe, I'm happiest when I know I'm headed back to the harbor of my dreams, especially when it's cold outside.

February 28

The days are getting longer now. February is passing. By the end of the month we are searching the trees for the first sign of swollen buds that indicate the coming of new, young leaves. Another season will soon be here, accompanied by bright colored flowers, blossoms and birds.

I retreat into my condo in February to enjoy my simple country pleasures. I always have a number of projects going. I'm usually knitting a couple of sweaters at once and have been working on the same embroidered sampler for the past eleven years, but I suppose completion doesn't have to be the bottom line. Occasionally I sew or sit down with a book or magazine, although most of my reading is done after I crawl into bed at night.

Probably my favorite pastime is putting things in order and cleaning things out, namely closets and drawers. I am forever amazed at the accumulation, so this is a task that is never finished, as by the time the whole house is sorted out, it's time to start again. With all these things going, time never gets heavy on

Winding Roads

my hands, not even in mid-winter.

One of the greatest rewards of condo living is the snug aloneness it offers, with good neighbors nearby. There is never an evening so snowy that a phone call won't bring a friend over for a cup of tea. The proximity of people when one lives alone is reassuring.

The stillness of a starry February night is just as encompassing here as it was on my grandfather's farm. The same stars that shine on me now shone on me then. So little changes, and yet so much is different.

Winding Roads

Chapter

3

March

March 1

When I awoke this morning, a wet snow was falling. The streets were passable, but the snow clung to winter's beauty on the tree branches and rooftops. It was a peaceful sight, and those of us who had no need to go out could sit back and enjoy it until it thawed. Surely this was winter's last blast.

March is the most fickle month of the year. It cannot make up its mind. One day we are lying on the deck soaking up the sun, famished for its warmth. A few days later the wind slaps the sleet against the windows like the crack of a pirate's whip. One thing we know for certain: winter's back has been broken, and spring is on the way.

We have had enough cold weather, and the first faint signs of spring are more than a month away. The sun hides behind a rush of gray clouds, and temperatures stay below freezing. Flurries of snow swirl about in the cold sunshine of the

Winding Roads

New England winter. In the brittle, biting cold of late winter, our faltering spirits long for a change so we decided to buck the weather and go for tea at a seaside inn.

Tea, which is one of the most charming pastimes in England, is enjoying a renaissance in America. The fare is lighter than that of the English high tea, and gone are the white gloves and hats that created the charming ambiance for this occasion abroad, but the Old World atmosphere still clings to the tea room.

When we arrived at the inn, the mahogany tea tables were set near the fire that blazed at one end of the room. From there we could look through the French doors leading onto the terrace and see the forsaken waters of Long Island Sound.

Our table was laid with frosty white, lace-trimmed place mats. The silver glistened, and the tea cups were transparent. I felt like Eloise at the Plaza. We were two children playing a childhood game. Everything was make-believe.

In true American fashion, the serving table offered a silver urn of hot water and a wide selection of tea bags. The fare consisted of homemade cookies and scones with clotted cream and marmalade, so delicious they would make the most seasoned Anglophile jump for joy. Surrounded by the glistening dark woods of the English furniture, we felt as if we were in Devon.

We lingered over our tea and biscuits for an hour and a half, and everything they say about tea is true. We forgot about the wintry weather, the economy, and all the other problems that are magnified by endless dreary days. We were carried away on a feather into a fantasy world that no longer exists. We floated freely in our opulent, stress-free surroundings, set against the dainty chatter and delicate laughter of ladies taking their afternoon tea.

Winding Roads

This brief respite from the world as we know it cleansed our souls and drew from our bodies the invisible poisons that accumulate there. Away from the noise and clamor of life, we were refreshed and renewed. We spoke softly and more slowly. We languished in thoughts of kindness as befitted our gracious surroundings. Moments like these are too few and far between, because we are too busy to find them. We rarely take time to indulge ourselves.

We stood in the heavy twilight gazing at the lights along the shore, caught in the magical moment when the world fades away and the horizon drifts across the sea. We returned to the tedium of existence with a brighter outlook and a far greater tolerance. Surrounded by beauty, we carried it with us when we left.

March 8

As winter ground to a halt, I brightened my home with a grandfather's clock. I bought it from a Connecticut clockmaker, which gives it a special sense of belonging.

In a condo if you bring in something new, it means getting rid of something old. I decided to get rid of a console stereo I had had for a number of years when I found the perfect place for the clock to stand. I donated it to a local agency, and it was gone by delivery day. The clock chimes in my living room. The chimes radiate an ethereal warmth throughout the house. They punctuate the most frantic day with tranquility. They echo the peace and dignity of yesteryear. This particular clock is a reproduction of an 18th century Willard clock and has the

Winding Roads

magical power to pull me back into the 1700s when, in our dreams at least, voices were softer, families were closer, and life was better.

Of course, it wasn't all that good. There was no running water, no central heat, electricity or antibiotics. People died young and often. Sewage was out of control in city streets, and massacres were common in the outlying areas. The truth is these clocks might be the best thing that's left from the colonial period.

Perhaps the clock's chimes arouse other memories as well. I remember visiting my mother's friends as a little girl, sitting primly in a formal living room and hearing the chimes of such a clock emanating from another part of the house.

Bored by adult conversation, I let my mind wander dreamily as I tried to envision the room where the clock was located. I would picture a grand entrance hall with a winding staircase, the clock against one of the walls. Or I would imagine it at the end of a long carpeted hallway that led to the back of the house. Or perhaps it was in a stately, highly polished dining room, or a paneled library filled with leather-bound books where the world seemed far away and everything was still. I went through the entire house in my mind, room by room, and passed the time until my mother was ready to leave.

I'm sure these memories of chiming clocks never left me, but my clock is in plain view. Nothing is left to the imagination. I have no entrance hall with winding stairs or library where the clock can exist in the aura it creates. However, several rooms away in my dining room an antique clock of my mother's has Westminster chimes. Perhaps some day a child will sit primly in my living room and her imagination will be stirred as mine was by the chimes of an unseen clock.

March 15

March is a transitional month. The wind blows hard and cold, and many of its days bring flurries and snowfall. We page through the seed catalogues, dreaming about July and August. The colorful descriptions of the roses and shrubs are particularly appealing when the sleet is scratching at the window. We are hungry for summer.

Since I have no garden, I have no seed catalogue. We have beautiful flowering shrubs, and many of us put spring bulbs into the ground when we moved here a few years ago, but I never got beyond that. Neighbors plant colorful annuals every year, and I miss the tantalizing fragrance of my French lilacs and the colorful day lilies that bloomed all summer long. There is room here for both, but I haven't gotten around to planting them. My outdoor work is confined to filling in the holes the dog digs that give my yard a mysterious gopher-like appearance.

March 21

Like many people these days, I'm always trying to figure out ways to simplify my life and my lifestyle. How did living become so complicated, and when did it happen?

Certainly life for the homemaker (if such a person still exists) has never been easier, but as modern conveniences set the woman free, she needed something to fill her leisure time, so she decided to have a career to help pay for all the modern conveniences. She finds herself juggling household duties, office, and motherhood. Also, the more modern conveniences we own, the more we have to repair and maintain. These machines are both a blessing and a curse.

Reflecting back to my grandfather's farm, I recall that his wife spent most of her time getting food on the table, sweeping the floors with a broom, and sewing on a treadle machine. However, she probably spent less time canning and preserving food in the summer than the average housewife spends in the supermarket in the course of the year. She didn't dash out for a can of mushrooms or some exotic ingredient for the evening meal. Recipes were simpler then.

Now it is impossible to pick up a cook book or a newspaper without a recipe that calls for a couple of odd-ball ingredients that will never be used again, the remains of which will be discarded. This is known as "gourmet" cooking. Almost everything is drenched in sauces that obliterate the taste of the food that is hidden underneath, be it asparagus or chicken breast. I like to taste what I'm eating, and the simpler the preparation, the better I like it. Cooking has become unaccountably complicated, which further complicates shopping and meal planning.

Leisure-time activities also vie for our attention. There are too many options. There are plays to see, concerts to attend, lectures, movies, bazaars, and benefits. In addition to this, we have a choice of an indecent number of channels on our thirty-two-inch televisions, not to mention the movies that are available for rent. Top this with organizational involvement, committee meetings, and volunteer work, and we soon discover that there is no such thing as leisure time in which we may pursue a personal interest or a hobby.

Winding Roads

The automobile has complicated our lives as well. First of all, there is the decision of make and model, and we are confronted by thousands of choices. When automobiles became easier to drive, people began using them more. The traffic build-up increases every day. We can jump into our cars and go anywhere at any time. The supermarkets are open 24 hours a day, and most of the shopping centers and malls are there to serve us seven days a week. Shopping is an unconfined leisure activity.

This March I am making a resolution to simplify my life. I will begin in the kitchen. Tonight I will fix a pot roast with onion soup mix, served with mashed potatoes and gravy. I will bake a custard pie for dessert. No one will have to guess what he or she is eating.

I will simplify my "errands" which seem to take up half of every day, by making lists and combining my trips, hopefully reducing "errands" to one day a week. That way I can spend more time doing the things I enjoy at home.

Dining out will be confined to two meals a week. Social activities will be limited to seeing the shows or attending the concerts that are really important to me. I will stop being overwhelmed by choices and possibilities.

I will return to the country pleasures of sunsets and walks by the river. I will learn to say "no" and slow down my life so I will have time to enjoy everything I do. I will stop racing through each day in order to get to the next. Let the winds of March blow away the bad habits of the past and sweep clean the slate of my life so that I may start with a new approach to a more peaceful style of country living.

March 24

We took our first walk along the shore today. The smell of the sea and the cadence of the waves made us aware of the timelessness of the universe. The boundless scope of the ocean puts everything into its place. The day was warm, but the biting wind that came in off the water reminded us that spring is not yet here. The late day sun glistened like pearls on the colorless, gray water as we walked in step like soldiers with our arms around each other.

The first walk on the beach in early spring has a special significance. It marks the psychological end of winter. It represents an emancipation from our homes where we have been imprisoned by the cold weather and the snow. It is approached with a spirit of freedom. We feel recklessly alive and unencumbered.

Other couples walking side-by-side or hand-in-hand smiled and spoke when we met. There is a common bond between us as we savor the emptiness of the ragged, endless shoreline. We are Neptune's children.

March 27

It is said that in a year's time most of us will make more appointments, see more things, meet more people, and go more places than our great-grandparents did in a lifetime. Being busy has become synonymous with success; being overbooked signifies "stardom." We have pushed ourselves as far as we can go.

Winding Roads

I'm thinking about life in the mid-19th century. Our country was less than 100 years old with a constantly growing population arriving from Ireland, England and Europe. This was the land of opportunity. Our cities in the East, especially those on the coast such as New York, Boston and Philadelphia, were growing by leaps and bounds. Charleston, Savannah and New Orleans were flourishing in the South. A land-hungry population was pushing west by covered wagon or flatboat to settle in Indiana, Illinois and Kentucky.

Since mass production and factories had not as yet gained momentum in the cities, agriculture was the leading occupation, so by far the greatest majority of people lived in the rural areas. Because travel was slow and uncomfortable, either by horseback or buggy, the early settlers seldom went more than a few miles from home. If family came to visit from ten miles away, they stayed for several days, bringing with them news from afar and returning with news from their trip. It was a pleasant exchange that usually took place in the kitchen, which was the heart of the house. A "visit" was exactly that — a time for sitting and talking and enjoying each other's company.

The men worked long hours and hard, clearing the land, planting the crops and harvesting, spending most of their time in the open fields under the blue sky where there was no crowding or pushing. Their ears were not deafened by the noise of machinery or cars; they heard only the lowing of cattle, the cry of a crow, or the sound of water rushing past in a nearby stream. Milking 20 cows before dawn was a relaxing chore when a man could be alone as the sun came up. Cows, like seedlings, cannot be rushed.

Women spent most of their time in the kitchen. When they were not preparing meals for their large families, they were

Winding Roads

canning or baking or getting the eggs ready for market. They got their fresh air and exercise when they worked in their gardens or hung the laundry on a line in the yard to dry.

Except for a christening, a wedding, or a wake, social life centered around the church, provided there was one within a five-mile range. Everyone looked forward to the "preaching" on Sunday. Those who traveled to get to the little church frequently spent the rest of the day with friends who lived nearby. Sunday was a joyful day of pleasure. No one toiled on the Sabbath. As for their chosen denomination, they were content to be whatever the nearest church required.

Certainly the hardships were plentiful, but they faced them as a unit and rallied around each other. Children died of typhoid, scarlet fever and influenza. Tuberculosis was a killer that couldn't be stopped. Fortunes were at the mercy of droughts and floods. Grasshoppers or locusts could destroy their crops, while hawks got their chickens if the fox didn't get there first. An inopportune hailstorm could wipe out a year's work in an hour. However, none of their threats were manmade. Most of ours are.

If the children were lucky, they had a one-room schoolhouse a mile or two away. After-school activities consisted of pumping water from the well, filling the kerosene lamps, chopping wood, or carrying feed to the livestock through the snow. In their free time they could skate on the frozen pond, wage an apple war in the orchard, or carve a piece of wood into a soldier. They used their imaginations and created their own games and activities. Our children need to be set free from too many planned activities and television, to dream, and to do.

Life has accelerated at a dizzying pace. Speed has become a tyrant. In 1860 a letter from "home" might take a month or

Winding Roads

more to reach the settler in Indiana; we have instant communication with any place in the world. We keep in close touch with our family by phone or electronic mail. When we get together on holidays, there is nothing to talk about that we haven't already heard. We don't sit down and "visit." We watch a game instead.

We have moved to the cities in droves. After working all week, Sunday is spent shopping or doing the laundry. We no longer have one day set aside to rest, and we need this respite more than we ever did, but time and economic pressures will not allow it. We get our fresh air on a crowded beach once or twice a year. We sit in front of the television to download. How far can we go in the direction of speed before the world has a nervous breakdown? How many choices can be put before us to fill every minute of our time before we short-circuit the earth and crash to a stop?

When I look back over my lifetime, I realize that the things that gave me the greatest pleasure were those I did with my hands, whether I was making doll house furniture or a dress, or knitting a sweater for a grandchild. Each stitch or each stroke seemed to be a mark in time, creating a new object from a piece of wood or fabric. These things also represented a quiet, unrushed period in my life. Creativity, I have decided, is what it's all about.

March 30

The cobwebs of winter are blown away once the windows are opened in spring. The balmy air and the sunshine

Winding Roads

make everything fresh and young again. The house stirs and breathes deeply. I lie on the deck in the afternoon sun and make frequent trips to the nursery to prepare my potted patio "garden" for the season ahead. At last, winter is over!

Chapter

4

April

April 1

The air has taken a turn for the better, and spring is on the way. The cats have been aroused from their winter slumber, and they are willing to leave the comfort of the couch to spend more time outside. They watch the birds at the feeder, but they're too old, and too indifferent, to attack. The birds, in fact, are far more aggressive and can frequently be heard screeching at the cats as they prowl around close to the ground, hoping not to be seen.

In spite of the changeable weather in April, the temperature ups and downs and torrential rain mixed with occasional wet snow, the spring flowers burst through the soil and bloom. The tulips, hyacinths and jonquils will soon pierce the drabness of winter with color and life.

April Fool's Day reminds us that April is the time to smile. If one picture is worth a thousand words, an afternoon of laughter is worth twenty hours of therapy. There is no underestimating the value of laughter in our lives. It is a key ingredient to our good health and our emotional well-being.

The first Sunday after I moved into my condo, I was carrying loads of packing trash to the curb to be picked up the next day when I crossed paths with my new next-door neighbor, a tall, handsome insurance executive.

"This is enough to make me get married again," I grumbled as I dragged my cardboard boxes behind me. There was a dead silence. Then in a humorless voice, he acknowledged my observation with, "Uh huh" and went into the house. It pays to know your audience.

My mother didn't have a sense of humor, but if we told her something was funny, she'd laugh as hard as anybody. She was just a little slow on the cues.

Once when we were visiting her in St. Louis, she took me aside and said she had something she had to tell me. She said a terrible thing had happened.

"What?" I asked, not noticing any disastrous changes.

"Well, last Christmas . . ." she began.

"Mother, that's nine months ago. Why didn't you tell me sooner?"

"I couldn't talk about it," my mother said. It seems she was Christmas shopping in one of the major department stores. Everything was jingle bells and jolly. Christmas carols were playing over the speaker system, filling the store with merriment and spirit. Everyone was happy.

My mother was riding up one of the escalators when she emitted a sneeze with such force that her upper plate flew out of her mouth and sailed through the store, coming to rest on the glove counter to the tune of "Joy to the World." I could imagine

Winding Roads

the startled look on the faces of the ladies downstairs when my mother's teeth missiled over their heads. Best of all must have been the shocked surprise registered by those standing at the glove counter when my mother's smile dropped in on them, but my mother wasn't there.

As I began to laugh, my mother saw the humor in the situation and joined me. The pain and embarrassment were gone.

"The awful thing was," my mother continued through gales of laughter, "I had to go down there and get them." After that, she was the life of every party when she told her tooth story.

Laughter is nature's face lift. Every time we laugh, our facial muscles pull upward. Laughter keeps us young. Stress and tension disappear. Not only do our faces pull upward when we laugh, but all our vital organs get a lift as well. It encourages our immune systems to perform in the manner in which they are expected. It is the best remedy there is for whatever ails us at the moment.

Once we see the humor in a situation, we have mastered it. Anger is displaced, and we have found a coping tool. Until that time, our negative responses are taking a toll on our bodies and emotions. Laughter is our key to survival.

Laughter is just as important as exercise. Many of us make sure we work out these days or run our five miles before work in the morning, but taking time to laugh should be another priority. Whether it's an hour of sit-coms in the evening, or re-runs of "I Love Lucy," we all need to find the emotional release that only laughter can bring.

April 3

Cats are territorial. They mark the perimeter of the property where they live; they mark the shrubs and their "special places." When we were living in the house, my cats would not allow another cat to step foot into our yard. They were similarly driven out if they tried to trespass in the territory that belonged to another cat. The fur would fly over the slightest violation.

Then we moved into the condo, and my cats were two of thirteen in the immediate area. The cat who arrived first had established his territory by the time we moved in, which included our yard, so when my cats went out, there were a couple of howling, yowling fights. As more people moved in and the cat population exploded, the boss cat gave up and started staying on the other side of the street. He couldn't keep twelve cats in line. However, the cats in our immediate vicinity have surrendered their territorial instinct. It is not unusual to see four or five of them in the yard together. Their acceptance of communal condo living is unnatural. Maybe somebody read them the by-laws.

April 9

In the course of doing my family genealogy, I met by mail a fourth cousin named Nancy. Nancy lives alone on a farm in the Blue Ridge Mountains of southern Virginia. After a divorce, she decided to give up teaching, and she moved into a little house in

Winding Roads

the country left to her by her father to pursue a self-sufficient, Thoreau-like existence.

She raises all her own food. She works long days in the fields, does her own planting, plowing and reaping. She has electricity and running water, but she lives without a television, a newspaper, or a refrigerator. She heats and cooks with wood and splits the logs herself. She is a cross between Scarlet O'Hara and Abraham Lincoln.

My best friend Phyllis and I frequently talk about simplifying our lives. When my alarm system threw a rod, my vacuum cleaner began shooting out fur balls bigger than the cat that had left them behind, and a spoon got stuck in the garbage disposal, I thought about Nancy and her simple existence.

About this time Nancy, who lives more than a mile from her nearest neighbor, called to say that she was awakened one night by the smell of cigarette smoke outside her bedroom window. A couple of days later she came home from town and found a cigarette ground out in the gravel of her driveway. That night she was sitting up late reading when her dog bristled and growled for an hour. With my urban mentality, it sounded to me as though she was being stalked. After a couple more incidents, she finally called the sheriff. A month later she said whoever or whatever it was, it was gone. She believed it was a bear or a raccoon. I didn't know they smoked.

When I asked her how she made out last winter, she said she kept busy bringing in wood to keep the stoves going and cooking three meals a day from scratch. Then the toilet froze, and a rabid raccoon jumped from a tree onto her dog, so the dog was quarantined for three months. Simplification was taking on overtones of inconvenience. I hadn't planned on taking it that far.

Nancy's daughter, a farmer's apprentice in North

Winding Roads

Carolina, had built a cabin on Nancy's property about a half a mile away from Nancy's house, and she sold it to Nancy.

"It's a cute little place," Nancy said, "Twenty-six by eighteen feet, with a loft." The living room in my condo is bigger than that.

"She lived there a year," Nancy continued, "but it doesn't have electricity or water." Nancy said she planned to run electricity to it from her barn, and add a chemical toilet.

"I figure it will make a nice little guest house," Nancy said in her charming voice that falls on the ear with antebellum beauty.

Phyllis and I have spoken of going to visit Nancy to see how we, too, could simplify our lives, but we are afraid of parking garages, so we certainly couldn't stay in the hills in a guest house with no dishwasher, a rabid dog, and a pot-smoking bear.

Nancy's life, we decided, is just as complicated as ours, but in a different way. It was a tough call, but we opted for our conveniences like plumbing, electric garage doors, and the microwave. Compared to rabies and stalkers, it didn't sound so bad. Simplification can wait until I take my shower, blow dry my hair, and finish the laundry. Furthermore, I can't drink warm milk, and I don't want my eggs hatching on the shelf. I kissed my fridge good night and went to bed.

April 16

Occasionally my best friend, whom we shall call "Marsha," drops an oar when she's at the helm, so I don't let her

Winding Roads

steer too often. Actually, her name is not Marsha, but I didn't want to jeopardize her chances of ever making another friend again, because she is basically a fine person, when she doesn't get out of control.

It all began on a Sunday afternoon. We were going shopping for curtains. I have gone "shopping" with Marsha on a number of occasions, and I have yet to see her buy anything. It reminds me of my friends who go "antiquing" three times a week but always come home empty-handed. They aren't "shopping;" they're "looking." Like Marsha, they engage the sales personnel in long conversations about their problems and needs, and after listening to a number of professional solutions, they nod approvingly and say they will have to go home and "think it over."

I, on the other hand, am a "direct" shopper. When I leave the house, I know exactly what I want, the color, the size and the quantity. I don't need the advice of a sales person who, in many instances, has been employed there for less than a month. When I find what I need, I buy it and leave. Shopping for me is a necessity, not a career.

Marsha and I got into my car. Ten miles from home, she remembered that she had left her wallpaper at my house, so we had to go back. Since she was looking for plain white curtains, I didn't know why the paper was crucial, but I didn't question it. Our plan was to visit three shops around the state, then have dinner at a quaint old inn in Avon.

Marsha bought nothing, but I found everything I was loking for, and we headed for the restaurant. It was early, so they showed us the lighter tavern menu. Among its offerings were meat loaf with mushroom gravy and garlic mashed potatoes, both of which are "trendy" again.

"Wow! Meat loaf and garlic potatoes," I said above the growling of my empty stomach. "That sounds good."

"Ecccch," Marsha grimaced between clenched teeth. "My mother told us never to order meat loaf in a restaurant."

I can remember my mother saying the same thing, but that was fifty years ago before refrigeration was perfected, and the Health Department was created.

"And who ever heard of garlic in mashed potatoes?" she asked. I wondered how long it had been since she had eaten out. "Let's get out of here," she suggested as she headed for the door. Wistfully, I took one last look at the wide floor boards, the soft lights and the worm-eaten chestnut beams in the ceiling.

Once in the car, Marsha suggested a family place in Farmington where she had dragged me once before, but I declined. I had dressed for Avon Old Farms, and I wasn't going to eat at a counter.

"I know," Marsha exclaimed in a moment of inspiration. "My in-laws used to rave about this place in _____ (a town of no significance whatsoever). Everybody says their food is wonderful."

"I've never heard of anyone going to _____ to eat, but if you know how to get there, we'll go if it's that great." I had my doubts already. I was hoping she couldn't find it.

But find it we did. It sat right on the highway like a truck stop, the name emblazoned in neon. Marsha said again that her in-laws always ate there. Not wishing to cast aspersions on the dead, I trailed in behind her.

When we went through the door, we were confronted by half a flight of stairs covered with soiled gold carpeting that I'm sure her in-laws must have tread upon some time back. We were seated in a poorly lit room, the decor of which pre-dated God. It was a blend of Early-Death and Late-Filth. The lack of lighting and the dark colors were violently depressing, as were the waitresses, the hostess, and the other diners.

"How well did you know your in-laws?" I asked cautiously. "When did they die? It was probably from eating here."

Let's see, I guess they've been gone for about twenty-five years now, but everybody says it's a wonderful place to eat."

The waitress poured well water into our thick amber glasses, and set down a bowl of fritters which we devoured ravenously. Then she brought an assortment of relishes, and some crackers. Marsha, her enthusiasm unwavering, slapped a cottage cheese creation on a cracker, took one bite, gagged and spit it out into her purse. She called the waitress and told her there was something wrong with the cheese, but the waitress smiled and said everyone else was eating it.

We ordered chicken cordon bleu, but they were out of it, so we had roast pork. I had melon for an appetizer, and Marsha had tomato juice (they came with the meal). She told the waitress her juice didn't taste right either. The lady suggested that maybe Marsha had used a strange mouth wash that morning.

Our salad was straight from a plastic bag, abundant, but tasteless. We didn't eat it (it came with the meal). A half an hour later our food arrived, huge hunks of dried out hog, drenched in gravy, mashed potatoes (no garlic) and carrots. The meat had some kind of indigestible casing on it like it came from a tube. I ate some of the potatoes and gnawed on a bit of the pork to give me the strength to drive home, but Marsha ate nothing, insisting everything tasted like mildew. I couldn't vouch for this, since I've

Winding Roads

never eaten mildew.

When the waitress saw all the food we had left, she offered us doggy bags. We told her not to bother. She removed our dishes, and at a nearby station, she carefully scraped all the meat onto one plate and carried it back into the kitchen. The rest of our remains became garbage, but I shudder to think that the meat was recycled.

After turning down dessert (it came with the meal), we paid the check and left.

"Marsha," I said, "I'm curious. Who are all these people who recommended that place to you?" It turned out it was one woman from her office, and Marsha didn't even know her last name.

I have a firm rule now: never listen to anyone who doesn't know more than you do. From here on in, I pick the restaurant.

April 20

When I was little and we attended a Protestant church, we were decked out in all new clothes for Easter Sunday. This was *de rigeuer*. Weeks of planning and deliberation went into the selection of this outfit. It began with a new pair of black patent leather shoes. Above these went a dress in the most fashionable spring color, a "topper" or coat in an eggy pastel, an empty purse, and an Easter hat we would never put on our heads again. When services were over, everyone congregated on the sidewalk and complimented each other on their outfits.

By the time we were teenagers, we chose our own clothes,

Winding Roads

striving for a sophistication we had not yet achieved. Out from under parental supervision, we went to sunrise services in the park. Although we had done our nails the night before, preparations began at 5 o'clock in the morning when we did our hair, our make-up and dressed. We walked to the bus stop where we met our friends in the darkness. All of us were wearing four-inch heeled shoes which our mothers said would turn us into cripples before we thirty. *Au contraire*, our feet seemed to thrive on the abuse.

In the chill of daybreak we stood in the park, oblivious to the service, but thrilled by the beauty of the sunrise. When the worshippers disbanded, we went to one of our favorite hang-outs for breakfast, arriving home in time to leave for services with our parents.

The dress code in the Midwest was rigid. No one wore a felt hat after Easter until autumn. Black patent leather could only be worn until Memorial Day, and white could not be worn after Labor Day. Velvet was fashionable until New Year's, at which time we switched to pastel wool. Silk, satin and velvet were fine in cold weather, but only cotton, organdy or voile was correct in the summer. No one ever wore black or white to a wedding. Black was for funerals or wakes. White was for the bride, not the guests. The penalty for breaking any of these rules was exclusion. Like our mothers, we were slaves to peer opinion.

Achieving maturity, I stopped buying a particular outfit for a particular occasion. Chances were it wouldn't be appropriate for anything else. When I see something I like, I get it, and when an occasion comes up, I wear something I already have.

I never wear anything the first time for a special event. That includes Easter, weddings or social affairs. I break in my clothes like a new car or a new pair of shoes. By wearing a new outfit in a neutral environment first, such as to church or the library, I feel more comfortable in it when I have some place special to go. It takes away the newness and sets me free. Most of the things I buy now are multi-purpose. I'm in for the long haul.

April 22

If you have a buffet or a china closet in your dining room, chances are you have a problem. It's the drawer where we say, "I'll just stick it in here for now." When the drawer will no longer open, we beat the contents down with a stick, and carry on.

I am a congenital "organizer." I like to know what I have, and where it is. My affliction isn't quite compulsive, but it is chronic. I never finish. Then, when I go to look for something, I can't find it. I'll never understand this.

In the process of my annual "springing," I finally tackled the drawer in the china closet, after cleaning around it for the past twenty years.

While this may not be of great interest to anyone, it might present a challenge. Here is what I found:

Six silver iced tea spoons, tarnished

Forty-two candles, some used, some bent, all soiled. I threw 17 of them away, but I'm ready for the next power outage. I can light up my house like a castle.

An ornate brass pendulum from an antique clock

Crayons, of course, from when the children were little (they're 40 now)

Two cameras with cases, a pair of binoculars, a hand-held tv, a car phone, and all the accessories for a knitting machine I

Winding Roads

never used.

Music and a cover for a keyboard that is a mystery, since I don't own one.

Forty-one birthday candles, none of which match, and fourteen unmatched candle holders.

A silver letter opener

A box of drapery hooks

A pair of black wrought iron sconces

Two flea collars

A dozen pieces of wood that have come off the dining room furniture, and one strip I don't recognize

Three votive candles

Place cards for formal dinners

A great picture of my two best friends, Wally and Vince, sailing somewhere in the Atlantic, taken before all three of us had stomach surgery

A plastic ruler that says "Go Navy"

Two boxes of Christmas tree lights

A sealed plastic vial of murky, white fluid, unlabeled

A bag of elephant clamps

A deck of playing cards from West Point

Sixteen batteries, assorted sizes

Two automatic timers for lamps

A box of single-edged razor blades with holder

A wrench

Four empty bags

By the time I sorted everything out and threw away a third of it, I was ready to put things back. I lined the drawer with Contact and began. The amazing thing was that it no longer fit. I had to put the two timers in the garage. This is one for Einstein.

Winding Roads

How can less take up more room that a lot? Is there a compactness in disarray that order precludes? But, never mind. At least I know where the binoculars are.

April 26

Arbor Day is recognized on April 26. The first Arbor Day, a day set apart and dedicated to tree planting, was celebrated in Nebraska on April 10, 1872. On that day one million trees were planted in the state. Six hundred million trees were planted there during the next sixteen years, and within twenty years one hundred thousand acres of the vast Nebraska wasteland had been turned into forests. The program is credited to a newspaper publisher, J. Sterling Morton, to enrich the soil, conserve moisture, and to provide windbreaks across the open stretches of plains in the Midwest. In 1885 the date of Arbor Day was changed to April 22, Morton's birthday, and it became a legal holiday in Nebraska. Now it is quietly observed in all the states and most of Canada.

Trees are frequently planted to commemorate special events or in memory of famous people. Birthday trees are sometimes planted when a child is born. The tree's growth is believed to indicate how the child will grow, but this is not necessarily true. My father planted a tree in our yard in Alton, Illinois, when I was born. The house was subsequently sold, and the new owners cut the tree down, but I'm still standing.

Winding Roads

April 28

How do we measure what we have? This question was put to me by my best friend Phyllis when we were touring the Vandervilt mansion in Hyde Park. Certainly this tasteless, ostentatious display of wealth brought no lasting happiness to the Commodore's heirs. They measured what they had in art work, gold leaf, European antiques and tapestries, overlooking many of life's most important treasures.

Phyllis and I agreed that we would rather have good health than gold leaf. If we adhere to a health-giving diet, an occasional forbidden treat will taste that much better. By the same token, our mental diet should be similarly selected with care. Our minds cannot survive on negative input. We must supplement the bad news with good experiences, happy moments and enrichment. These are vitamins for our emotions and help keep our perspective on track.

We wouldn't trade our friends and our families for all the European antiques in every Vanderbilt mansion still standing. One good friend is worth more than all the Louis Quatorze in captivity. The outpouring of love that we give to our families and receive in return cannot be bought or bargained for. These are treasures of the heart.

Our modest homes are compensation enough for the art work and tapestries in a marble mansion. We came by our possessions with more love than money. Each object in our homes is filled with memories — a gift from a grandchild, or a fragile reminder of a marriage that was ended by death. My home holds me securely in its warmth. I am safe and protected here. When I open the door, it welcomes my friends and shelters my noisy, laughing grandchildren. Sometimes my house is filled with conversation and laughter, but when everyone leaves, and I am alone, I bask in the peace and silence that restore my soul. A mansion cannot enfold a family the way a cottage can.

We have shelter, clothing and food, the basics of existence. Once these basic needs are met, their repeated enhancement can add to our net worth, but our happiness does not increase proportionately. Phyllis and I have learned to be satisfied with what we have, the first step on the road to contentment. We are no longer competing with a consumer-oriented society. Peace of mind is an intangible treasure.

We don't have to win Lotto. Phyllis and I are "millionaires" many times over.

Chapter

5

May

May 6

As the days lengthen, I frequently drive to the river after dinner to watch the sun set. It's only five minutes away. The Connecticut River is one of the cleanest in the state, so it sparkles in the late-day sun. It's peaceful there and quiet. The ferry boat that plies the river throughout the day is tied up at the dock, marking the early evening with the slap of water against its old wooden sides. Seagulls skim the surface in flight. When I get home, I walk the dog at twilight. These are the joys of early summer.

May 9

Memories, blown by the breeze, rush through my mind

when I am relaxing on the deck of my condo. The sound of young green leaves brushing against each other in the gentle wind reminds me of the relief this offered on a hot afternoon in Missouri. In the Midwest where trees do not proliferate as they do in New England, the farmer always planted a ring of trees around the house as protection against the burning sun of summer and the stinging winds of winter. However, the breezes were not as frequent there as they are here, so a day when a breeze rippled the trees was a special day, one to be relished and enjoyed.

Only now in retrospect do I realize that this breeze was important to us as children as well. We didn't feel the heat the way our parents and grandparents did perhaps, but we knew when we were uncomfortable. The sound of the breeze brings back the memory of those trees around the house and the comfort they represented. We sat in the mottled shade with our dolls and listened to its song. As I hear the wind brushing through the trees that edge our property, I escape back to childhood and those Midwestern summers when a breeze signified a good day for playing.

May 12

All my good intentions and my languid country lifestyle erupted into a frenzy of activity the first of May, when I went to Long Island with my son to look for a place for him to live. Reluctantly I waved good-bye to my little house and nosed toward the highway that would take me to New York City.

Long Island is an unknown quantity to anyone in Minneapolis, San Francisco, or Seattle. Long Island is just off the

Winding Roads

coast of New York, connected to Manhattan by bridges. Both Queens and Brooklyn are on the Island, but because they are boroughs of the metropolitan New York area, they are not considered a part of Long Island per se.

Long Island consists of two counties, Naussau and Suffolk, popular commuting locations that make them a long arm of New York City itself. It is the overflow basin for New Yorkers who want to leave the city for a more suburban lifestyle but stay within the shadow of its skyline. The island is 130 miles long from the Big Apple to Montauk Point, and its greatest width is only 20 miles. It lies in the Atlantic Ocean parallel to the "gold coast" of Connecticut, but it can only be reached from that state either by driving west into the city and backtracking east on the Long Island Expressway or by ferryboat from three points on Connecticut's southern shore. There are no bridges from Connecticut to Long Island.

Over 2,775,000 people live on the Island, and two-thirds of them work there. It wasn't until after World War II, and particularly in the last twenty years, that the rural character of the Island gave way to suburbia. The southern shore at the eastern end of the Island has a smaller year-round population and is a popular resort area known as the Hamptons. The entire length of coast on the south shore is lined with barrier beaches, while the north shore on Long Island Sound is more rugged and caters to boaters.

On the way down, after more than an hour of battling crowded highways and road repairs, while trying to connect between one thruway and the other, I turned off permaturely and found myself in South Bronx. Once off the highway in these heavily populated urban areas, it is impossible to get back on again. I went into a bank and got directions from one of the customers. When I crossed the bridge into Queens and got onto the Long Island Expressway, my nerves were shattered by the traffic and the speed with which the cars were moving. The trip took three hours from my home in Connecticut.

We settled into a motel next to the expressway. After lunch we went out with a real estate agent to look at houses and apartments. Since the island is sandy, we didn't see any buildings over four stories tall. The apartments were all in private homes. Some of the residential neighborhoods were magnificent with deep, green lawns, flowering shrubs, and blossoming trees. The trend was toward contemporary architecture. I knew I had left Connecticut.

Our search continued the next day, the result being that my son found a large apartment in a beautiful residential area in a town called Dix Hills in the middle of the island, about 15 minutes from where he would be working.

I came home on Sunday morning when traffic was light. This time I missed a freeway connection again and wound up under the highway with a motorcycle rally. There must have been at least 1,500 bikes down there, reaching as far as the eye could see. I circled and circled, but I was caught in a loop. Finally I emerged into a residential district in Queens. It took me 15 minutes and the help of the police to get back on the highway. For a while I thought I might have to buy a house and live there, since I didn't believe I would ever find my way out of the maze of narrow streets that seemed to lead nowhere.

Anyone who has been on the corporate trail and moved every few years knows how customs and lifestyles vary from one part of the country to the other, from one state to the next, or even from town to town. Like most islanders, Long Islanders are insulated from the rest of the country. Most of them have lived there all their lives, and the majority of those who move there come out from New York City. With a broad industrial diversification, the Island has a high employment rate, and it takes care of its own. Only a small number of people, like my son, come to the Island in a career move, but most of the people who live there stay there all their lives. Young people live at home until they are married. If they didn't, they couldn't afford to buy a house on Long Island later.

I was looking forward to exploring the Island more fully and spending a good part of my summer on its broad, sandy beaches, but before my son finished unpacking, his company moved him to Philadelphia. I never got to the Hamptons.

May 16

May is a delight for a number of reasons. It is warm enough to open the windows and let the fresh air blow through the house but not hot enough to need air conditioning when the windows must be closed again. It is the one month that we can touch and feel with every fiber. We experience it in the beautiful flowering shrubs, the azaleas, the spring tulips, jonquils and hyacinths, and the blossoms on the trees. The curtains flow like dancers in front of the open windows. The sun is warm, but the shade is cool. It is a perfect month.

May also brings us fresh asparagus, rhubarb, and California strawberries, all of which are synonymous with spring. Nutritionists maintain that we should always eat foods that are in season. No matter where we live in America now, due to our transportation system and refrigeration, we can have foods

Winding Roads

like canteloupe, avocados, or grapes year-round, if we don't mind paying the price. However, the nutritionists advise against these indulgences, recommending that we eat seasonal foods, preferably home-grown in that part of the country where we live. Years ago we could mark the changing seasons by the greengrocers. In winter we ate root vegetables and hard squash. While bananas were imported throughout the year, the only other fruit we had in winter were apples, oranges and grapefruit.

We didn't need a calendar to know it was spring when we saw the first home-grown asparagus or strawberries in the store. As the season progressed into summer, we were deluged with local produce — corn on the cob, green beans, lima beans, tomatoes, leaf lettuce, cucumbers and peppers. Melons began showing up in early July. Seedless grapes, rosy peaches, apricots, plums and pears highlighted our summer. The nutritionists tell us now that eating five portions of fresh fruits and vegetables daily will keep cholesterol down. They also recommend that we eat three to five nuts every day, and fatty fish such as salmon, tuna or sardines, twice a week. All the rules have changed.

May 21

Unlike my grandfather's farm, my country condo is in Utopia. The lawns are like velvet, and a weed doesn't stand a chance. Little green men spray chemicals all summer. The shrubs are bedded, and the trees are bug-free. The mosquito population has been decimated, and the stinging insects wiped out. There's nothing to swat within two miles of my back door.

I sometimes wonder about this. It's like living in isolation, no insects, no pests, and therefore no birds because there's nothing for them to eat here. I miss the chirping of the birds, and sometimes the silence is spine-chilling. While the mosquitos at my grandfather's farm were not much fun, the buzzing of the bees and wasps in the flower gardens sang the song of summer. We thought of them in terms of honey. They had a purpose and we knew it. Honey in those days came in the comb. There were several beekeepers in the area who sold it. My mother would bring it home and place the comb in a bowl so we could eat the sweet, golden drippings on homemade bread. I find it difficult to accept the yellow syrup in a jar as "honey," even though I don't have to see the cow at the table to trust the milk.

Our Utopia is a showplace with its breathtaking beauty, but sometimes I feel as if nature is out there waiting to get even. I haven't seen a housefly for two years now.

May 22

Mother's Day is a day when we enjoy being with our families, particularly our mothers, or our children, but this isn't always possible. Circumstances change, people move away, young people are transferred, and we have to learn to be creative with our holidays to avoid those dismal holiday blues.

We found that the best antidote for loneliness at these times was to break with tradition. When our sons were away, my husband and I enjoyed champagne brunch on Christmas at West Point, or we had Christmas dinner at a hotel, sometimes alone, sometimes with friends. These occasions were very festive, and certainly no one knows better how to decorate for the holidays than the hotels. We were cast in with other people like ourselves.

Winding Roads

The people who work in these restaurants on Christmas Day make it a rare treat indeed. We didn't feel sorry for ourselves or anybody else who was eating there. Everyone was having a jolly time.

One year we took our son and daughter-in-law to Plymouth, Massachusetts, for Thanksgiving. We saw the fascinating sights of Plymouth and had a traditional Thanksgiving dinner at the community hall where it was served family style on long plank tables.

On another occasion when the children were little and Mother's Day rolled around, I didn't want to face the crowded restaurants when they offered to take me out for dinner, and I didn't want to stand in the kitchen cooking, so we piled into the car and went to Salem, Massachusetts, where we visited all the witch haunts. The children loved it. Mother's Day dinner was burger and fries at a fast-food place. We avoided the crowds, saw many new things and had a delightful experience.

This year when Mother's Day arrived, I had to work. I was a theater critic and I was scheduled to cover a show at the other end of the state. A friend of mine met me there, and after the show we ate Chinese at a nearby restaurant, again avoiding the crowds. One of my sons had been relocated, and the other one wanted to work on his boat, so nobody was offended, and I had a great day with an old friend.

These unusual outings take the sting out of the lonelines of holidays. It's adventuresome and just a little bizarre. Traditions, like rules, are made to be broken.

Winding Roads

May 30

Decoration Day used to be May 30. I believe it still is. In the small town in Illinois where I was raised, that was the day we went to the cemetery and decorated the graves of our family with huge bouquets of cut flowers from our yard. The highlight of the day was a parade in memory of all the men who had died in war. Many veterans of World War I marched in the parade, and each year we watched the number of Civil War and Spanish American War veterans dwindle, until a sole survivor was pushed in a wheel chair. I can remember my excitement over the parade as a little girl, because it meant I could get a helium-filled balloon and a box of Cracker Jack with a prize in it. Treats such as this did not come often during the Depression.

When many of the holidays were shifted to Monday, Decoration Day was phased out and became Memorial Day instead. The purpose and the meaning were the same; only the name and the date were changed.

To this day I cannot pass up the Memorial Day parade, although I have lost my passion for both balloons and Cracker Jack. I attended last year's parade in Old Wethersfield, Connecticut, a town that is steeped in history. Settled in 1634, Wethersfield is one of the oldest towns in the state and boasts a number of houses that pre-date the American Revolution, the most outstanding of which is the Webb house on Main Street where George Washington met with Comte de Rochambeau in 1781. That house and several others have achieved museum status. Certainly there could be no more appropriate place to hold a Memorial Day parade.

Winding Roads

May 31

If we walk in the footprints of nature, we rejoice in the rebirth of spring. As the pale green leaves burst forth on the trees and break through the brown winter soil, we are swept away on the swell of new beginnings. The pastel colors of the season awaken us to the miraculous possibility of rewriting our lives. Now is the time.

With pen in hand, we assess where we are and where we would like to be, bearing in mind that all things are possible. As we awaken from winter's hibernation, shedding scarves and boots and coats like an animal loses its polar fur, we emerge from our hearthside hideaway with new hope, new life, and new resolutions. Spring is the start of our spiritual year.

We are inspired to lose weight, change the style or the color of our hair, and buy new clothes that capture the person we'd like to be and the impression we want to make. This in itself is a release. We feel new again, like the bright yellow flowers in the garden of life. It is the first step in the process of "becoming."

Next we look at our surroundings. Maybe it's time to refurbish, to bring the awakening of spring inside our home with something as simple as a vase of pastel-perfect silk flowers that quickly turn a room into a garden. Or maybe the time has come to think about moving to that cabin in the woods or the small apartment with a view of the water. To achieve such earthly happiness, everyone must find where he or she "belongs." Many of us are there already, but spring is the time to broaden our vision and perhaps change our horizons.

The final consideration in our springtime rebirth is bringing the newness of life into everyday living. We do this by

Winding Roads

trying new things, going new places, learning new skills, and meeting new people. It is the only answer to stagnation. Our friends are those who make us try harder and do better. Like the ugly duckling, we must seek out the swans, as we will be our best among our own kind.

So we begin the new year patterned by nature. Our body rhythm falls quite naturally into place. We instill newness into our lives, which inspires growth. We take our place in the universe with a new stride and a fresh outlook. After we make a few changes, we are ready to sprout bright blooms like the tulips and the hyacinths, adding our gift of beauty to a troubled world. With it we bring inspiration to others. Like flowers that bloom on a battlefield, neither beauty nor blossoms can be stopped by circumstances.

Winding Roads

Chapter 6

June

June 4

Why is it winter seems to stay forever and summer rushes by so fast? We've been to the shore to watch the sun set and the full moon rise from the rooftop terrace at the Castle in Old Saybrook. With an open vista over the water, the sun sets in ribbons of iridescent color; the rising moon dances on the waves.

We've visited Water's Edge in Westbrook on warm summer evenings, then walked the beach after dinner. We've had lunch at the sidewalk cafe in Glastonbury and on the terrace at the Blacksmith Tavern. We've visited the gardens in Coventry and basked in the peace that reigns there. We managed to do a salty day in Newport where we ate on the wharf at the Black Pearl and sat next to the sea as it pounded without mercy on the boulders that line the shore.

Winding Roads

As for a vacation, we haven't made any plans, because we can't decide which of the beckoning places to visit. We are torn between the Outer Banks, Bar Harbor (with a ferry boat ride to Nova Scotia), Appalachia, or a trip back to Illinois and Missouri. We usually wind up staying home because we wait too long to decide where to go.

This gives me the opportunity to discover that many of the joys of summer can be experienced at home. The table bows under the bountiful supply of local produce, and farm stands are abundant. The best salads of the year come from these crisp, freshly picked vegetables, and the tomatoes are sun-baked red and fragrant. We bypass the grapefruit in favor of local canteloupe and pass on bananas to indulge in blueberries, peaches and plums.

The roses are in bloom, as are the long-necked day lilies. Gardens are a fragrant canvas of flowers and color. Honeysuckle and moon vines climb the trellises, and the lawns are still green from spring rain. Sitting in the shade of a protective tree on a hot afternoon with a soft breeze blowing is as good as it gets. In the evening I enjoy relaxing on the porch in the glider with a book in my lap where I usually read until dark or until I feel the first mosquito chewing on my ankle.

The shore is just thirty minutes away, and the mountains are less than an hour's drive in the other direction. There's ice cream in the freezer and lemonade on the table. There are concerts in the park and restaurants to pleasure any taste. The days are warm, but the nights are cool. We can sleep late in the morning without missing the breakfast call or a tour bus that will take us to see the sights. We live at our own leisurely pace. There is no need to hurry or keep to someone else's schedule.

I find everything right here. When I walk outside on my deck in the fresh, early morning air, I am overwhelmed by the

Winding Roads

fragrance and beauty of the flowers that are growing there. If I were to walk out on the same deck in Italy or San Francisco, I would say, "How charming! How lovely!" Since it's my deck in Rocky Hill, I glance around and say nothing. The same beauty we find abroad can be found in our own back yard, but it takes on a greater magnitude when we have traveled so far to see it.

The other night after the theater we stopped for a bite to eat at a sidewalk cafe near the river. It was a warm evening with a soft breeze that dispelled the humidity. Had it been in Paris or Rio, we would have gasped with ecstasy, but because we here within ten miles of home, we took it for granted.

We had seen a marvellous, new, one-man show at an unusual, intimate, little theater two stories below the earth's surface in downtown Hartford. We could have been in Greenwich Village, or London, but we have it right here.

When we went to see a show at the Goodspeed Theater in the old Victorian building on the banks of the Connecticut River, we had dinner on the terrace before the performance. Had everyone not been speaking English, we could have been sitting in a beer garden on the Rhine.

No sunset anywhere can compare with the ones we have seen over Long Island Sound. The wide-angled scope of the vista, the powerful colors that fill the western sky, and the soft, sweet smell of the sea create unforgettable moments that we forget all too quickly because they are so close to home. A similar sunset anywhere else in the world we would talk about for years. Parts and pieces of everywhere could be anywhere else. Places, like life, are repetitions of past performances. Everything is an encore.

Wherever we go, the same lazy clouds float overhead in a pale blue sky. It may be a little grayer in London than it is in Palm Beach, but we are all under one roof. We can shuffle our feet and

Winding Roads

head for the far corners of the world, but when we get there, we will say, "Doesn't this remind you of . . . . "

Certainly New England has more to offer than we can absorb in a lifetime. True, there are certain attractions that can only be seen on site, such as Mt. Vesuvius, the Grand Canyon, or Niagara Falls; otherwise most places look pretty much the same, no matter where we go. When we are at home, we can imagine we're some place else and save a lot of money on the trip.

June 7

Home has always been where my heart is. When I was a little girl, my ambition was to grow up and be a housewife. I thought there could be nothing nicer than to be home all day doing the things our mothers did, like housework, baking, sewing, or reading magazines.

This summer I am finally realizing that dream come true. I am a housewife. The first thing I did was empty a basket of ironing that had been sitting in the closet for a little over two years. I thrilled to the sizzle of the steam and gloried in the reassuring smell of slightly scorched cotton.

Then I set aside one day a week to bake. I made cookies for my grandchildren, froze a few pastries for unexpected guests, and tried a couple of new recipes. However, when I gained seven pounds, I eliminated that program from my plan.

I had friends in for brunch, holiday picnics, and small, intimate suppers. It was nice to have time to entertain, and visit with my favorite people. Then I gnawed on TV dinners when I was alone.

I planted seventeen pots on my desk with flowers — zinnias, impatiens, geraniums, pansies, snap dragons, and petunias. In four more pots the size of buckets, I grew tomato plants that are loaded with fruit. If this experiment is successful, next year I might try corn or canteloupe.

I then made a dress for my granddaughter and considered making one for myself, but the moment had passed so I picked up my knitting instead and turned out an afghan. I have done all the wonderful things I had always dreamed of doing, and now I don't have to do them again.

The most rewarding thing this respite has allowed me to do is spend long summer evenings of lingering twilight sitting on the deck, listening to the bird calls, and watching the condo cats frolicking on the lawn. The younger ones somersault in the air in pursuit of an unseen enemy. The senior cats lie lethargically in the dew-drenched gass, and watch.

I thumb through *Lear's* until the light of the day dims below the distant horizon. This is when I leash up the dog, and we take our daily walk in those beautiful, crystal-clear, quiet evening hours on a perfect summer night. By the time we return, the fireflies are sending starry signals I cannot understand, but the sparkle of light at the edge of the woods transmits a universal message of hope.

In Illinois where I grew up, all the houses had front porches. Some of them were screened. They were "multi-purpose" rooms. Almost every porch had a swing or a glider and a couple of rocking chairs. We children played there in the afternoon while my grandmother rocked back and forth hulling peas or beans for the evening meal.

Winding Roads

After dinner people sat on their front porches and talked quietly. Conversation tinkled like the ice in the lemonade. Occasionally friends or relatives would drop by, and they, too, would be entertained on the front porch with a cool drink, or a piece of cake. It was a friendly, relaxed place to be.

After World War II, the front porch was replaced by the patio in the back of the house, but this did not serve the same purpose. Entertaining on the patio meant preparing hors d'oeuvres and drinks. Ice-cold watermelon and lemonade were at home on the front porch. The patio lacked the friendly feeling of enclosure that we enjoyed on the porch, so the deck came into fashion. The deck falls somewhere between the front porch and the patio, although it is usually found in the back of the house. Nevertheless, it is attached to, and is a part of, the house, and it has a floor and railings to separate it from the yard. It seems to belong to the house more than the patio does. The deck has boundaries that provide a form of insulation without obstructing the view.

My deck is my "front porch." From it I can see the street or the woods in back of my house. It's the best of both worlds. My dog Phoebe and my two cats stretch out languidly on the cool boards beside me, their heads turning in unison each time they hear an unfamiliar sound.

As I sit there enjoying my country summer, I am reminded of the lowing of the cattle at sunset, and I think about the farmer, something we rarely do. Every morning he has to milk the cows, whether he feels like it or not. He has no choice. It's not like brushing your teeth or flossing. You can't skip a day, and do it twice the next night. Those cows have to be milked at sunrise and sunset. Be it blizzard or heat wave, pneumonia or chronic fatigue, the bovines have to be thoroughly milked, and there are no shortcuts.

It's not just the cows. The milk, once drawn, has to be processed and prepared for market. The pigs have to eat, although they're not too fussy, and there may be sheep or horses to round up or stall. There's no time off for good behavior. The animals must be milked and cared for every single day. This goes on day in and day out. The farmer never gets a break, no two weeks with pay, and no sick leave.

Of course, some of the farmer's duties, such as milking, have been automated, but the cows can't hook themselves up to these machines. The farmer still has to be there to keep things running, so to speak.

In the summer when the farmer drags out of bed at 4:00 in the morning, at least he has the joy of the sunrise and the sound of the rooster crowing his wake-up call. The grass around him sparkles with dew. Buttercups and wild flowers dot the fields and meadows as they raise their sleepy heads to the glory of a new day. Everything springs to life in the golden rays of dawn.

Nevertheless, it is a non-stop, year-round responsibility that lasts until the farmer is 75 or 80 and sells out to move into town. He can't go to Disney World or take a mid-winter cruise to Bermuda. In fact, if he visits his cousin in the next county, he has to be back by sunset.

We can leave the dishes in the sink until the cows come home, but when they do, the farmer better be there to meet them. In spite of the pressures of his work, I've never seen a stressed-out farmer.

Winding Roads

June 16

Here in Rocky Hill life on the river hasn't changed much since Huckleberry Finn was rafting on the Mississippi. The same serenity that water inspires, augmented by nature's colorful pallet, still exists.

Water has always been an important part of our history. In the early days of our country's founding, when the first settlers began arriving in America, the large cities mushroomed along the banks of a navigational river, since water transportation was the best available at the time. The first major metropolitan areas were the seaports that welcomed settlers from Europe: Boston, New York and Philadelphia. These new Americans fanned out through new England, upstate New York, and across Pennsylvania, hence to Virginia, and the Ohio River where many of them traveled west on flat boats, thus giving birth to cities like Cincinnati, and St. Louis. Rivers have played a major part in the development of our country, and while the focus may have shifted over the years, rivers still have an esteemed place in our lives.

Since Rocky Hill isn't a major tourist attraction, only the natives visit our park on the river, a small site carved from the wooded area that lines the banks of the Connecticut River. It is from this point that the oldest continuously operating ferry boat in America drifts lazily back and forth across the water between our town and South Glastonbury on the other side, leaving silver ripples in its wake. The pace is languid and long-ago. The ferry transports three or four cars on its deck, and, since it is part of state highway 160, it carries cyclists with their bikes, hikers, and sightseers.

Winding Roads

On the other side, the road winds through rich lowlands dotted with horse farms, and tobacco sheds. The old homes are jewels in colorful floral settings. The tree-shaded road leads through the countryside until it comes to Main Street in South Glastonbury. The green fields and orchards stretch as far as the eye can see against a backdrop of the gentle Glastonbury hills.

I like to visit the park in the morning when the sea gulls are sunning themselves on the boat launch. They lie there in the warmth of the sun, completely content, with none of the cares that plague the higher species such as man. It seems to me those sea gulls know something we should learn.

The park welcomes everyone. I frequently stop there when I am running a multitude of errands. If I sit in silence for fifteen minutes or a half an hour with nothing but the chatter of the sea gulls for company, my metabolism slows to the pace of the flowing water. It is impossible to feel hurried or harassed while gazing at the distant green hills or the rippling water that reflects a flawless summer sky. The river whispers to the shore. It says, "Slow down . . . slow down . . . slow down."

June 23

What shall we have to eat? I recently came across my mother's recipe book from the 1920s that was put together by a chapter of the Eastern Star in Alton, Illinois, where I was born. In those days everything was made from items the average housewife had on the shelf. If she wanted to prepare something from a cook book, she didn't have to make a mad dash to the grocery store for eye of newt, frog's wort, or East Indian spices, items she would never use again and could ill afford to throw

Winding Roads

away.

Strong spices were originally used in the Mediterranean countries and warm climates where food spoiled quickly because they concealed the taste of spoilage. "Gourmet cooks" use them freely now, since they have become readily available, and they are necessary, not because of spoilage, but to replace the natural taste of our food that has been lost through chemicalization. When I was little, a good canteloupe was the size of a baseball. Now they are the size of footballs. As size increases, flavor is stretched. Only in a health food store where the fruits and vegetables are organically grown can you still find the real thing and the real flavor. These vegetables and fruits are smaller than those in the super market and have less eye appeal since they have not been ripened by gas, nor have they been dyed or waxed, but the flavor is outstanding.

The recipes in this little book were before the time of the kitchen helpers we have now. Stoves did not have thermostats, and all the beating and mixing was done by hand. Outside of the occasional use of onion or garlic, the main spice was Cayenne pepper, although a few other spices, such as cinnamon, sage and nutmeg, were available at that time.

The ads in the Eastern Star cook book are as interesting as the recipes. The Ozier Beautye Shoppe offers "shingling, bobbing and marcelling." Another ad is by "C.J. Jacoby & Co. - Complete Home Furnishers and Undertakers — We welcome you to call and inspect our displays."

Measurements and instructions for preparing the dishes featured in the book are casual, if not altogether vague, such as "two shakes of pepper," "a medium size bottle of stuffed olives," and "a good sized bunch of celery," or "two rounding teaspoonfuls baking powder." The ingredients for buttermilk biscuits are "Lard the size of a walnut, thimbleful of soda, 1 coffee

Winding Roads

cup buttermilk, 2 quarts flour, bake until browned."

Among its entries are recipes for *Baked Potato, Boiled Potatoes,* and four different versions of *Mashed Potatoes.*

There is a recipe for *Macaroni Soup* that gives the ingredients but doesn't mention cooking. There are a number of recipes for sandwiches, each of which instructs the maker to put one slice of bread on top of the other.

One of my favorite recipes is for *Head Cheese (good)* which says, "Take one pig's head, clean and wash thoroughly, removing eyes, nostrils, ears. Singe and wash again. Boil until meat...."

There is a special section entitled *The Invalid's Tray.* This consists of recipes for such things as flaxseed lemonade, chicken jelly, boiled beef pulp, broiled oysters, albumenized milk, milk pap and milk gruel. *Bon appetit!*

June 29

The temperatures occasionally hit the 90-degree mark in June, but after several days of refrigeration, my system rebels, and I turn off the air conditioning. I want to get in touch with summer again. The windows are open, and a stiff breeze blows through the house. It feels like summer is supposed to.

This is what it was like before we had air conditioning. We put on a pair of shorts with a sleeveless tee shirt and enjoyed the weather. With modern methods it is difficult to tell the seasons apart. I find myself sleeping under the same blankets in the summer as I do in winter and, in fact, wearing many of the same clothes. This isn't right. Once in a while we should experience a change in the weather.

The upstairs gets warm when the afternoon sun beats down on the roof, but not nearly as warm as the upstairs used to get at my grandfather's farm where insulation was unheard of. In the heat of those days we would seek quiet repose on one of the feather beds in the afternoon, the idea being that sleep would make the night come sooner. The summer heat was part of our lives. We accepted it and dressed for it.

For one day it is part of my life, and I am enjoying it. Turning off the air conditioner is like a trip down memory lane, but I am happy to know I can turn it back on whenever I choose. Usually there is a light breeze that blows up from the shore sweeping the heat of the day out of the house like a new broom. As the warm day draws to a close, darkness spreads on cat's feet, like Carl Sandburg's fog, silently and still. The only sound to be heard is the chirping of birds as they make their last calls of the day. Finally the trees are silhouetted against the gun metal gray of the sky, and Venus erupts in the west.

June 30

Country evenings in June are long, luxurious twilights of relaxation. It isn't necessary to be in the country to enjoy "country evenings." I recreate my country evenings by sitting in the glider on the deck until dark. Nothing gets done in the evening in June, but it's not supposed to. This is the time to luxuriate in the early summer season before the heat gets serious but after all the chill is gone from the air.

Winding Roads

    Everything slows down in the gathering twilight as the stress of the day gives way to the mysterious beauty of the night. Voices become softer as we release the cares of the afternoon. Stress seems far away. It is a time to relish. The work is done, dinner is over, and the golden hours of evening spread out before us like a fan.

    Occasionally the evening skies cloud over, and a clap of thunder sends us hurrying inside. There is no roof over the deck, so I can't watch the storms from the porch as I did in Illinois. Summer thunderstorms, while not as common in New England as in the Midwest, herald a change in weather. The lightening dances across the sky, and the rain comes down in torrents. When the storm is over and the rain stops falling, lightening bugs weave patterns of whimsy as they dart through the woods, iridescent diamonds sparkling on a quilt of velvet darkness, and another country evening comes to a quiet close.

Winding Roads

Chapter 7

July

July 1

I can still taste the cold fried chicken, the potato salad, angel food cake, black cherries and Kool-Aid that my mother fixed for picnics when we were little. To me it is the only picnic fare worth bothering with. Picnics were meant to be shared with the ants, and ants don't like imported cheese, crab meat or spilled claret. They'll take sweet, sticky Kool-Aid every time.

Certainly July, with its hot days and warm nights, is the height of the picnic season in New England. We picnic in the parks, at the beach or on waves of grass in open fields. We picnic on our patios and in our back yards. The menu may have changed, but the spirit has not. This is the essence of summer.

Our summers are short and must be savored to the fullest in the least possible time. Each day is precious. So we pack up a lunch and head for the beach where we eat on a blanket with sand in our food, a small inconvenience compared to the beauty of the breeze blowing in off the clear blue water, or the sound of the surf on the shore. Too soon the day is over, and it is time to load the car and go home. We cling to July like the tail of a kite, staying aloft in its breezes as long as we can, holding tightly to the elusive warmth of a hot summer day. If only July could last until October!

July 4

When I lived in Missouri Fourth of July marked the midway point through our long summer. The oppressive heat and humidity began early in April and lasted through the end of September. It was not unusual for the temperature to be over 100 degrees when we went back to school in the fall.

The annual Fourth of July parade is no longer held in many major cities, but these wonderful, patriotic celebrations can still be found in small towns throughout the country, a practice that is unfailingly upheld and supported in Connecticut.

When I attended a parade in a nearby town, I was shocked to see how few people stood when the flag passed by. Everyone should stand and take a moment to think about what that flag means to each of us who live here. Rising and removing one's hat are acts of respect and allegiance to our flag and our country.

The Revolutionary War that brought about the birth of

our nation took place only two centuries ago. We are still a young country when one looks at the history of Europe and the battles that have been fought there. We study the Revolution when we are in school, but only history majors give it much thought after that.

We lose sight of what many of our forefathers, our fourth or fifth great-grandparents, went through to gain this coveted freedom. We no longer relate to Washington's rag-tag troops, undernourished, poorly clothed, cold and hungry. They fought with their hearts as well as their hands. They wanted this country to be theirs. They were not in some far-off land because they had been sent there to preserve someone else's freedom; they had volunteered because they wanted to acquire it for themselves. They gave their limbs and lives for the very land they and their families lived upon. They suffered, not for glory, but for a cause. Freedom was gained inch by inch, hour by hour.

This is what the Fourth of July is all about. This is what we should recall as we observe all the fine people, young and old, who march in this parade. For those of us whose ancestors fought in the Revolutionary War, we are another link in the chain of Americans. Those who came later can also recall that it was this great war and its warriors who established the country that opened its gates to the oppressed, the downtrodden, and all the others who sought the same freedom that we enjoy here. The Fourth of July is everybody's holiday.

July 17

Nineteen-thirty-five wasn't a good year for anybody,

Winding Roads

except maybe Shirley Temple. It certainly wasn't one of my better years. I spent most of the time looking like a leper with sties on my eyes, first one eye, then the other. They were painful and uncomfortable, and the only relief was hot packs until they burst and the infection subsided. Worse than the pain, however, was my appearance, with one eye or the other always red and swollen shut.

My mother took me to the doctor who administered drops and ointments, none of which seemed related to the illness. Nothing helped. They gave me vitamins and cod liver oil and increased my intake of fresh fruits and vegetables. But the sties recurred with painful regularity.

The middle of July my mother packed my clothes into a suitcase for my annual three-week visit with my aunts in Illinois. Aunt Pearl and Aunt Grace were sisters. Aunt Pearl was a beautiful spinster. She had chestnut hair and a dimple in her cheek. She also had asthma and was in delicate health. Aunt Grace was a horse of another color. She was manic. She worked in the house from sun-up until bedtime, cleaning, scrubbing, cooking and polishing. She never stopped. Aunt Grace was married to Uncle Roy, the jolly kind of uncle one associates with Christmas.

The sisters squabbled constantly. They never agreed on anything. Aunt Pearl was aesthetic and charming. Aunt Grace was a drudge, but each in her own way had a heart of gold. While Aunt Pearl wrote poetry and acted in plays, Aunt Grace was up to her armpits in soapsuds. Aunt Grace and Uncle Roy were religious fundamentalists; Aunt Pearl read quietly from her Bible and prayed. Aunt Pearl looked for beauty and found it. Aunt Grace looked for work and did it. However, they were united in their love for me.

The third day I was there I felt the familiar soreness in my right eye, an indication that a new infection was about to erupt. I nestled in Aunt Pearl's arms for comfort, but the following morning the pain was intense. The sty still hadn't broken when I went to bed that night.

I hadn't been there long when Aunt Grace and Uncle Roy came into my room with four or five strangers. Startled, I sat up straight in the big double bed.

"What are you doing?" I asked with fear in my voice. The people in the room didn't speak. They circled the bed where I was lying.

"It's all right, honey," Aunt Grace said. "These people are from our church. We're going to pray for you and ask God to get rid of those sties on your eyes."

The people in the room began to chant softly, each wording his supplication in his own way. The words overlapped and displaced one another.

"Dear God, Jehovah," I heard my Uncle Roy say, "please take away this little child's suffering . . . ."

Please, Lord, heal this child . . . ."

Then Aunt Grace's voice wailed in a passionate plea, "Lordy, Lordy, heal Helen's eyes; take away the pain and the suffering . . . ."

"God, we pray that the sore on the child's eye will heal and that she will never have another. Please, God, heal this child . . . ."

With the swaying bodies hovered over me in the fading twilight, it was eerie and unnerving. I thought I was going to die.

"That's enough, Grace. You're upsetting her. Let her go to sleep," my Aunt Pearl said.

Winding Roads

I didn't think I would ever sleep again. The more I cried, the more painful my eye became. While everyone was praying for healing, I became worse and worse. Then the sty burst in the night. I was much better the next day, and I never had another one.

As the weeks went by and I looked back on that evening, I pondered the miracle that had taken place there. I told my mother that Aunt Grace and her friends had healed my sties by praying, but my mother said, "Don't be silly. You simply outgrew them." I didn't answer. Many years went by before I realized I had been touched by the hand of God, and I was healed.

July 19

We're having a "heat wave." The temperature has been over 90 degrees for six days in a row, and over 100 degrees for three. This warm weather makes front-page headlines, and every night it is the lead story on the evening news. It is blown out of all proportion. We are led to believe that this is an emergency situation that only the hardy will survive.

Life slows to a standstill. The streets are empty, traffic is light, and there is no one around. All seek refuge in their pools and their air conditioned homes. We have been psyched out by the press.

I can remember childhood summers in the Midwest that were much hotter than this, but life went on. Appointments were kept, everyone went to work, and it was business as usual. And there was no air conditioning in those days. We played in the shade in the back yard on the hot afternoons, and slept with an electric fan humming over our heads at night. Summer was expected to be hot. One-hundred-and-five-degree heat didn't make headlines.

Then there was the summer of 1951 when the temperature topped out at 115 degrees. It was like walking around inside a furnace. Admittedly, this heat made the front page, since many people died because of it. The press was so unfavorable that the official weather service thermometer was moved from the city to the airport, where it was at least ten degrees cooler, an attempt to lead the people in town to believe that they weren't as hot as they thought they were. Also, the true readings were hurting the tourist trade and affecting business. The best way to cool off the city was to move the thermometers out of town. Everyone felt better.

Along with the intense heat, we had grasshoppers, huge green insects with leaping legs that spit "tobacco." They were like a plague. They damaged crops and gardens, and could eat through canvas. Our yard was full of them, but I haven't seen one since I was little. I often wonder what happened to the grasshopper population. Perhaps they aren't indigenous to New England, but from the contacts I have made, I'm not sure they are abundant in the Midwest any more either. Maybe when they moved the thermometer in St. Louis, the grasshoppers went with it.

Summer became far more bearable with the advent of air conditioning, and our lives are hardly disrupted by the heat. We can go to a movie, eat in a restaurant, or shop in a mall in total comfort. Our clothes don't stick to our bodies when we ride in our air-conditioned cars. We can roast a chicken or bake a pie without heating up the house. The good old days are nice to

Winding Roads

remember, but modern living has its advantages.

July 27

We left Connecticut in late July to go to Maine, where our accommodations overlooked Frenchman's Bay in Bar Harbor on Mount Desert Island. We were staying on the site of the former estate of one of my favorite authors, the late Mary Roberts Rinehart, the popular mystery writer whose books we had discovered when we were teenagers. The eerie atmosphere that greeted us rekindled our intrigue with the past. The fog floated across the island like a phantom. The melancholy croak of a fog horn groaned through the muffled darkness. An iridescent halo glowed along the shoreline until it was once again darkened by the constantly shifting fog.

Mary Roberts Rinehart bought her Bar Harbor "cottage" in 1939. "Fairview," designed around a courtyard and surrounded by formal gardens and terraces, was built in 1909. The mansion, which was destroyed by the 1947 Bar Harbor fire, had a commanding view of the harbor. Its stone walls still stand and have been incorporated into the foundation of the rambling motel that is located there now. The fountain in the formal garden has become a planter, but the terraces with their showy flowers and the twisted trees that survived the flames remain much as they were then. From these fragments of yesterday, the grandeur of the past can be reconstructed in the mind.

Mary Roberts was born in 1876 in Pittsburgh, the daughter of a disenchanted sewing machine salesman. Both her parents met tragic deaths. Her father committed suicide, and her mother, partially paralyzed after his death, died as a result of an accident in which she was burned by boiling water.

Mary Roberts trained as a nurse, but four days after her graduation in 1896, she married Dr. Stanley Marshall Rinehart. When the young couple suffered financial setbacks in 1903, she sold her first story for $34, then went on to sell 345 more that same year, earning $1,800. Her first book, *The Circular Staircase*, was published in 1908. The book became a play and was performed in seven languages, grossing several million dollars.

From 1920 until her husband's death, Rinehart wrote three mystery novels, seven other novels, three books about her popular character "Tish," a play, eight romances, two collections of short stories, and her autobiography, which was published in 1931. She was the highest paid woman writer of her day.

After her husband died, she used her summer home in Bar Harbor for eight years before misfortune struck again, when her cook went berserk and tried to kill her. The cook later committed suicide, and the cottage was destroyed in the Bar Harbor fire in 1947. The prolific author of 61 books died in 1958 at the age of 82.

Bar Harbor became popular when it was discovered by the super rich in the latter part of the 19th century. Newport was already an established summer colony, but Bar Harbor offered an isolation that added to its elitism. Soon "cottages" similar to those in Newport, were being built along the Bar Harbor shore, mansions big enough to hold large families, their guests, and a retinue of servants. The majority of the members of the summer colony came from Boston, New York and Washington with an average of ten servants per family. These exclusive summer residents established their own private clubs where they enjoyed a stylish social life with one another.

After the turn of the century, when Bar Harbor became

more accessible by land transportation, a new influx of tourists arrived, staying at hotels and in guest houses. As the cottages became more expensive to maintain and the need for guest accommodations increased, several old mansions were razed or diverted to commercial use. The fire of 1947 was the final epitaph to Bar Harbor's Golden Era.

The fire, which destroyed one-third of the island, began on October 21, 1947, and became an inferno two days later when it was fanned by gale-force winds. Sweeping the length of Eden Street where many of the old mansions were located, it wiped out the west end of Bar Harbor, then roared through the gorge and over Champlain Mountain, finally burning out almost three weeks later at Thunder Hole in Acadia National Park. When the flames died, all that was left standing of the famous Bar Harbor cottages were their chimneys and stone foundations.

Although Mary Roberts Rinehart's presence is invisible at Fairview, it is undeniable. As we sat on the balcony enjoying the sweeping panorama of Frenchman's Bay, watching the sparkling tiers of lights on the Nova Scotia ferry returning to port in the darkness, we felt a strong kinship with the author.

July 28

We invariably come back from vacation asking, what's the hurry? What's all the rush about? Where are we going? And what will we do when we get there? How much can we squeeze out of each minute and each hour of the day?

I blame my computer for this confrontation. Like computers, everything keeps getting bigger, faster and more complicated. Electronics, which are incorporated into almost

Winding Roads

everything we do, drive, or even wear, are responsible. If we are to be part of the Electronic Age, and it is unavoidable, we are in a constant learning mode. Every time we purchase a new appliance, we have a new set of questionable instructions, frequently written by someone in Japan with only a small knowledge of English. Fortunately for everyone, these instructions come in three or four different languages to accommodate world distribution, so if English doesn't work, you might try German, or, if you are a linguistic intellectual, the original Japanese. Whether it's a VCR, a printer, a television or a washing machine, brain overload is just around the corner.

When you buy a new computer, it will become outmoded in six months to a year. No one wants the old one. Computers, for the most part, must be considered "disposable." I gave my first one to a friend who put it in a closet. My second one I passed on to my grandchildren who have politely but firmly turned down my third one because it's too slow, so now I have two, one upstairs and one downstairs. I'm not getting another one in the foreseeable future.

Instead, my son tells me, we are "upgrading" what I already have. Actually it suited me fine just the way it was, but I don't want to be left behind in the electronic dust of yesterday. He launched this project by upgrading my modem. This is the little hunk of wires that makes it possible to connect via telephone lines to the immediate world. It was a matter of replacing one small piece inside the computer with another. It took less than three minutes to accomplish. However, it took three hours to make all the internal adjustments through the keyboard to make everything jibe. I sat there groaning as my son jumped from screen to screen. I assuaged my fears by the fact that if he can work with nuclear power, presumably he isn't

Winding Roads

going to blow up my computer.

To give a non-computer person some idea of the difference the change made. I was using my original modem mainly on a service for electronic mail, a convenient way of keeping in touch as fast as a phone call, but at much less expense. The speed of the modem was measured as 2400 baud. I have no idea what that means, but the new modem he installed works at 33600 baud. However, the online computer services are operating only at 28800. They haven't reached 33600, so for once I am ahead of technology! I shall now wait for it to catch up with me, and when it gets here, I'll be ready.

The truth is I didn't mind the slow modem. It took a little longer, but I just sat back and relaxed while I waited. Now I'm on the edge of my chair trying to keep up with it. It has deprived me of my relaxation time. And while it runs much faster, the complicated system becomes more complicated every day, the result of internal enhancements, so this slows it down, and I'm not saving any money on the deal, which was supposed to be its major advantage.

Now I have access to the "Net" and World Wide Web. I had understood that this would allow me to use every library in the world, a great tool for research, but so far I haven't been able to get into one source. Instead, I get messages like "Overload — Undo," or, after an involved series of operations over which I have no control, "This file cannot be retrieved now — try again later, sucker." And I'm paying by the minute. I estimate it will take me approximately six years to learn how to use the Internet. In the meantime, somebody is going to come up with an easier way, so I believe I'll just wait until they do.

While I'm not ready to pound my laundry on the rocks, I sometimes find that the old-fashioned way is not only faster, but more reliable. I rarely get out my food processor to grate carrots or potatoes. By the time I get it out and put it together, cut the vegetables into acceptable strips, then clean up the mess I made, and put the processor back together again and return it to wherever it was, I can have the job done in less time on a hand grater.

I use my microwave for quick warm-ups and find that this is an expedient means of heating leftovers or TV dinners, but I do not cook meals or roast turkeys in it. According to the instruction book that is almost half the size of the family Bible, this timesaver will do any number of things that I don't need. We rarely use any of our modern conveniences to their capacity, because it takes too long to figure out how.

As for research, I go to the library where the atmosphere is conducive to deep thought and intellectual pursuit. I have never met anyone in the library's research department who wasn't eager to help. Some one will even do it by phone if I call in. I soon discovered that it takes less time to get into the car, drive to the library, and find what I am looking for than it does to get on the Net only to find out that what I want isn't available, so I have to go to the library anyway.

The interaction between my librarian and me is stimulating, as is my relationship with my hand grater. I have plenty of time, but I am very particular about how I use it. Nice people have far greater appeal for me than impersonal electronics ever will. I greatly miss the reassuring voice of a live telephone operator, another plunge down the tubes of human contact. It doesn't take long to realize that the timesaving automated phones take at least four times as long. What these devices say to me is, "Your time isn't as important as ours." Then we're put on "hold."

July 30

Summer is slipping away. August is just around the bend, bringing with it an urgency to do the things we have missed and visit the places we intended to go. We make mental plans as we bask in the heavy solitude of a July night, full of ideas and good intentions, but disinclined to get out of the hammock to look for a pencil.

The dark blue sky of a July night reflects our flag with its multitude of sparkling stars. It is symbolically more peaceful without the red stripes of blood and war, or the white stripes of death. May all the earth share in the peace of a star-studded July night.

Winding Roads

Chapter

8

August

August 4

In August we see the fading days of summer slipping through our fingers like water. The goldenrod and Queen Anne's lace signal the end of the season. The days are noticeably shorter, and the chill of autumn stalks the star-studded nights. Winter overstays its visit, and summer leaves too soon.

We think of all the things we didn't do. We didn't make that boat cruise to Sag Harbor, nor did we get to the Goodspeed Opera House this year. We meant to go to Lenox, Cape Cod and Nantucket. We wanted more hours at the shore and more time in the mountains. We had intended to follow some of the trails that lead through the woods to no place in particular and visit relatives down South. There is never enough time, and time is running out.

Winding Roads

August 7

    Where are the "meadows" of your mind? I read an article recently that said everyone should have "meadows of the mind," a visionary retreat where stress is forgotten and peace is restored.

    Most of our "meadows" go back to childhood, although we occasionally find a "meadow" in our grown-up world. All of our "meadows" are attuned to nature, places of serene beauty accompanied by the universal sounds of wildlife and weather. There are no manmade intrusions in our "meadows."

    One of my "meadows" is a deserted beach on the Outer Banks of North Carolina where the white, sandy seashore extends for over a hundred miles to the treacherous banks of Cape Hatteras. The rhythm of the pounding ocean as it crashes against the land is the heartbeat of eternity. It cannot be stopped; it cannot be changed. Its constancy is awesome, persisting through the millenniums and continuing through all generations to come.

    As I stand alone in this desert-sea, hungry water snatches at my feet. I watch the wide-winged, blue-gray gulls soaring and diving overhead, caw-calling to each other in a lonely, distant throttle. This is not a silent "meadow." My voice cannot be heard above the roar of the white-capped surf. Engulfed in this beauty and the wonder of the world, my tension and stress are swept out to sea, drawn from my body and my mind by each receding wave as it ebbs back into the fathoms of the earth's watery womb from which all life must come. Here I find tranquility in turmoil.

    Another meadow of my mind is the side of a hill on my grandfather's farm in Missouri where I used to lie on my back as a child, basking in the quiet abundance of the farm. I could see

Winding Roads

the horn-of-plenty vegetable garden edged by my grandmother's flowers. Beyond that was the orchard bursting with fruit that went into the golden-crusted pies that emerged from the oven of the kerosene stove in the kitchen. On down the hill were the black raspberry bushes, their bounty protected by the stickers and thorns that clawed at the intruder who reached for their riches.

Overhead in a satin-smooth sky rarely wrinkled by clouds, a hawk soars on the wind in silence. The sounds in this meadow are the tsk-tsking of green tobacco-spitting grasshoppers and the buzzing of beetles and bees. A melodic cacophony of bird calls and the hollow tapping of a woodpecker from a dead tree in the forest echo across the hills. The chickens cluck contentedly as they strut about the yard. Far-away voices carry from the house.

My third "meadow" is a cabin in the forest primeval on an island in Maine. The majestic pines become lacy silhouettes against the gray sky after the sun has set. Water splashes gently against the dock in the darkness, and the jagged cry of the loon accents my island isolation that brings me to terms with life. Here I withdraw into myself to seek that which I cannot find in the city. Staring hypnotically at the water that surrounds me, I assess my goals without prejudice or pressure and reaffirm my personal values. I am but a dot in the expansiveness of the flat landscape of the sea and the sand, but on the island in Maine I am the center of the universe.

Where are the "meadows" of your mind, those special places that enchant you with their memory?

Winding Roads

August 11

Remember all the little sayings our mothers and grandmothers used to tell us when we were small? Their ominous warnings were like witchcraft, and we believed every word.

My grandmother used to say, "Dream about the dead, and you'll be surprised by the living." Once when I dreamt about the dead, two days later I had to have a tooth pulled. After that if I dreamt about the dead, I sat there awaiting the catastrophe, and it invariably came. It took me a long time to realize that these things happen anyway, and they aren't brought on by the deceased. I used to hate to dream about the dead. It scared me. Now I find it rather comforting, seeing old friends again or being with my husband in my dreams. Time changes things.

Then there was, "Tell a Saturday night dream before breakfast, and it will come true." We always hoped for a wonderful dream on Saturday night so we could rush to the breakfast table and relate it, but I don't remember any of them coming to pass.

My mother used to say, "Once the rain starts, the danger from the wind is over." I learned differently when we lived in Kansas. The danger from the wind is never over. Most of our tornados were accompanied by rain.

My grandmother said steel attracted lightning, and she told me you had to cover anything made of steel during a storm. She would wrap a blanket around the sewing machine and hide the iron in a closet. A lot of people in the Midwest had something called "lightning rods" attached to the roofs of their houses. They looked like antennas. I believe the idea was that this would be the highest point, so the lightning would run down the lightning rod and be eaten up by the earth.

And how about "Lightning never strikes in the same place twice." Don't you believe it! We were hit three times in our house in Connecticut. The third time it happened, our insurance company made us put in a lot of ground wires and precautionary devices, since they were getting tired of it. So much for lightning.

I can remember my grandmother cautioning me not to count the number of cars in a funeral procession because that would be how many years before I died. Once she told me this, I had to fight to keep myself from counting the cars to see if it was really true. Or "Dream about a wedding, and there's going to be a funeral." That's right. There usually is . . . eventually.

My mother even had some bits of wisdom she passed on from her own grandmother, things about setting hens and cocks crowing, but I didn't retain them since we lived in the city, and these things were not part of our lives or our predictions.

Then there were "Sing before breakfast and you'll cry before dinner," "Pretty is as pretty does," "Bad luck comes in threes," and "Waste not, want not." Life was full of warnings and rules that were carved in stone.

It is amazing how many years it takes to outgrow some of the fears and superstitions that were acquired in childhood. We believed wholeheartedly everything the adult members of the family told us, and we weren't going to take any chances. Many adults still enjoy the good luck of a four-leafed clover or will walk around a ladder rather than under it.

There is no denying how important input is during these formative years while the children are still young enough to believe in the infallibility of their parents, the most important

Winding Roads

people in their lives. Their young minds are like empty pages, waiting to be written upon, and these early words will stay with them into adulthood, as will proper grammar if they hear it every day.

To this day I always crack a window on the leeward side of the house during a bad storm, and my roof hasn't blown off yet, but I stopped covering the sewing machine after the third lightening strike.

August 13

The zucchini attack should be ending soon. Once frost hits, we will be safe. Everybody in Connecticut grows zucchini, but nobody wants to eat it.

I was walking my dog yesterday when one of my good neighbors stopped me and asked if I like zucchini. This is a trick question, like "Do you like cats?" I should have known what was coming. People have been giving me zucchini all summer. I thanked her for the offer, but said I didn't want to strip her vines or deprive her. She said it was no problem, she had plenty, and she had four of them right there on the front porch already bagged. She was desperate, so I took them and thanked her.

How much squash can one person eat? How many loaves of zucchini bread can I give to my friends? What I really can't figure out is how people living in a condo can produce this much squash in an area less than four feet square. I wish they would give me money instead.

Winding Roads

August 14

We celebrated V-J Day August 14, 1945, with trepidation and certain reservations. Certainly we were happy the killing had ended and our prisoners would be released, but as terribly modern young ladies who knew little else but wartime and uniforms, we suspected our lives would drift back into the doldrums for which pre-war St. Louis was noted.

Far away from the coastlines that might be in danger of attack, we were not in touch with the slaughter that was taking place all over the world, and we had never heard of the gas furnaces in Germany. The frantic changes that took place because of the war signaled the end of the Depression and heralded a prosperity, the likes of which we had never seen before. Everybody had money again.

Our lives changed with the times. We were lifted out of the mediocrity that was our intended fate into a new world that came to us. St. Louis was filled with excitement and an air of expectancy. We felt snug and safe nestled between the plains and the mountains that protected us from the sea. We were not afraid. Before the enemy reached St. Louis, it would first have to conquer Oklahoma City or Indianapolis.

We lived with a minute-to-minute spontaneity amidst the crush of the men in uniform. The city was surrounded by military bases. There was a new face around every corner. The peacetime circle in which we had moved had no upward spiral. It just went around and around. There was little opportunity to meet new people, but then the war came along, giving us a chance to meet men from all over America. The war was an opportunity for growth and expansion. Everything had changed,

Winding Roads

and it would never be the same again.

Peacetime industries converted to wartime production. Salaries and wages skyrocketed. Rosie the Riveter was no laughing matter, and the "swing shift" was the place to be. We couldn't comprehend the horrors of war described in the newspaper headlines. We didn't experience the war or feel it, except as a side effect in our lives.

Raised in the obscure middle-class mediocrity of the Midwest, my sister and I were "Hollywood" children. We passed our childhood in the 1930s reading movie magazines that fueled our fires of discontent. We wanted to taste the excitement and glamor we found on the slick pages of our dreams. The war was our escape.

We didn't have air raid drills. We had no air raid shelters or blackout curtains. A few of our friends joined the newly formed women's branches of the service, but many more of them married their high school sweethearts in quickly planned weddings before their new husbands were sent overseas. Marine pilots were the pick of the litter. Next came Naval fliers, followed by Army Air Corps pilots (those who flew Mustangs were preferred over the ones who took to the shrapnel-skies in the more sedate B-17s or B-24s). Such was the pecking order of our hearts.

We could not comprehend the battles that had provided us with the liberties and opportunities that were unknown and forbidden in the Midwest until the bombs fell on Pearl Harbor. We wrote V-mail letters to our boy friends, and when they came home on leave, we dined in the finest restaurants. Every date was filled with the dramatic impact of the uncertain times. We went to pool parties where the guests

Winding Roads

were Naval Air Cadets; we enjoyed tea dancing at the Statler Hotel with French fliers; and mingled with G.I.s from all over the country at the U.S.O. Meanwhile, the letters flowed -- to the Pacific, to Europe, North Africa, and military installations throughout the United States.

We met servicemen wherever we went, all of whom were away from home and lonely. We wore fox "chubbies," or a string of squirrel pelts strung together and hung around our necks. Clothes were our passion.

The flip side of the war was rolling our own cigarettes, wearing rayon stockings that braided around our ankles and took two days to dry, and, worst of all, shoe rationing. We weren't bothered by gasoline rationing since none of us had a car.

When the war was in its fourth year, the defense plants were hitting peak production, and young men were being drafted as soon as they finished high school, but one sensed that things were winding down, a premonition we denied because of the stifling effect the changeover to peacetime pursuits would have on our lives. Although the excitement and urgency of a nation at war were still present and apparent, as victory in Europe drew nearer, G.I.s were beginning to think about the girl back home and the transition to civilian life. Change was in the wind. It was the beginning of the end of an era.

The war ended with V-J Day, and the men began returning home, thousands every month. The glamor was gone. Department-store mufti replaced bell bottoms. Pilots became insurance salesmen, and heroes went back to college. The urgency and excitement were missing. The worst years the tormented world has ever known, the most disastrous era in our country's history, were the best years of our lives.

Winding Roads

August 24

Earlier this week, one of my hundred-year-old cats left a bird on the back porch. The bird must have been handicapped, because these old cats can hardly find their own food bowls. I scooped it up in disgust and placed it in a paper bag in the garbage container in the garage.

Three hot days later, the odor was overwhelming. I had to get it out of there before it saturated the house, but where could I put it in this urban environment, without getting arrested for littering?

With the garage door standing open, I told my story to the man next door. He offered to put the paper bag full of bird into a plastic bag. He said that would contain the smell. He suggested, since it was mid-evening, I drive up to a dumpster and deposit it.

I didn't want to carry it inside my car, so Peter hooked it to the tailgate where it could flap along behind me. Certain that someone would see me tossing a dead bird into a dumpster where I didn't belong, I drove straight to the police station. At a traffic signal, the driver of the car next to me honked to tell me that there was something falling out of my trunk.

When I got to the station, I told the officer on duty that I had a dead bird in a plastic bag hanging from my tailgate that smelled so bad I had to get rid of it, but I didn't know where. I asked him what they do with roadkill. He was sympathetic to my problem and told me I could throw it in the dumpster by their back door. I thanked him.

Gingerly I removed the plastic bag from the tailgate and went to the dumpster, but it was six-feet tall with no doors, and it was piled at least eight feet high. There was no way I could toss the bird on top of all that was already there. If I tried to throw it up, I worried that it might fall back and land on me. If I overshot my target, I could be chasing it around the parking lot all night. It was like a bad dream.

Fortunately, at that moment another policeman came out of the building. "Officer," I said, "I can't get this bird on top of all that trash. It's too high." He directed me to a much lower and emptier dumpster around the corner. I pitched the bird in and got out of there, but when I drove past the station two days later, I noticed a pervasive odor . . . . .

August 26

The first rustling sounds of autumn can be heard in the dryness of the leaves and a symphony of cicadas singing in the trees. Their scratchy song is comforting in its annual repetition, a thread of continuity that is woven into the cloth of a lifetime.

The warning, rasping sound of the cicadas triggers any number of memories that go back as far as our earliest recollections. Since cicadas are found almost everywhere in the United States where deciduous trees abound, the memories they stir are spread across the country. There is hardly anyone who hears the cicadas of late summer who doesn't experience a flashback to another time.

Sometimes I hear my grandmother's voice in the call of the cicadas, drifting through an open window into the back yard where we were playing in the twilight. My grandmother was a wiry, little lady who hated the Roosevelts and the "Roosians." In fact, it was the antics of these two groups that kept her fiery and

Winding Roads

alive. She awoke each morning with great expectations of what either of them would do next. As the people in England are "royal watchers," so my grandmother followed every move the Roosevelts made. She could hold her own in any argument.

My strongest stirring when I hear the cicadas, however, goes back quite a few years to Kansas City. We moved into our home in a Kansas suburb on September 1. It was a French-style farm house, surrounded by trees. The stillness was overwhelming, but then the cicadas started. There must have been millions of them in every tree. They called all day and well into the night. We were new in the area, and their mournful cry enclosed me in a cage of loneliness.

Two years later when we were transferred to New York, I tried to duplicate this favorite wooden-roofed Kansas house in Connecticut, but, alas, the builders didn't know from weeping mortar, and we couldn't have a wooden shingled roof because there was no city water on our rustic lane. In spite of all my efforts to retain the French charm of my house in Kansas, it came out looking typically New England. You can't go home again, and you can't take it with you when you leave..

Cicadas also remind me of getting-ready-to-go-back-to-school days. This was a momentous time in a little kid's life. It meant trying on wool skirts and sweaters and winter coats in the stuffy dressing rooms of the downtown department stores. There was no air conditioning then. Only the excitement kept us from scratching our sweaty skin raw in those itchy clothes. The payoff was lunch in the tearoom or a hot dog at Woolworth's counter.

Back-to-school preparations included a new pair of "school shoes," a term that was synonymous with "ugly," and six pairs of socks, but the best came last. This was when we hit the dime store for the new school bag (our answer to the backpack,

Winding Roads

and the reason one of our arms will be forever longer than the other), a pencil box, a fresh box of crayons, and a lined tablet with an Indian on the cover. Outside of Christmas, it was the shopping spree of the year.

Sometimes if we were particularly patient and well behaved, we would be treated to a new piece of sheet music for the piano that we played with varying degrees of skill. Sheet music at that time was three pieces for $1, or 35 cents a piece.

Woolworth's and Kresge's were the biggest dealers in song. They carried all the current hits. There was a piano in their music department, and a pianist, usually a woman. She would play anything you wanted to hear. That was her job. Of course, she played it far better than we could ever hope to, but we believed that we would sound the way she did, so a sale was made. That lady was worth her weight in gold.

There weren't many piano players left at Kresge's or Woolworth's by the time we were teenagers, but there were one or two, and we knew where they were. We would go downtown with our friends on a Saturday afternoon and listen to the piano-lady play all our favorite songs for an hour or more, but we rarely bought anything, not even at 35 cents a shot.

With our thirst for music still unquenched, we would then head for the record department of a nearby department store, where they had private, glass-enclosed booths with lounge chairs and a record player where you could listen to any record you liked before you decided to buy it. We usually stayed until closing. Such were the inexpensive joys of our younger days.

In some remote way, these thoughts and recollections are tied together neatly by the sound of the cicadas as we embark upon a new season and resume our lives after a long summer vacation. The cicadas are always there to show us the way.

The cicadas are going to be around for a while, and I'll tell you why. Once fertilized, the female splits a leaf in which to deposit her eggs. When the little ones (called "nymphs") are born, they drop to the ground and burrow below where they feed on the juices of tree roots for up to 17 years before they emerge to take their place in the kingdom on earth. Chances are they will be there to bring back memories for our grandchildren and their grandchildren, and that's good to know.

August 31

August is almost a memory. The fireflies have turned out their lights and gone home. The days are getting shorter. The cheerful conversation of the cicadas and the rustling of the leaves in the trees tell us that fall is just around the corner.

Here in New England we glory in the changing seasons and the startling variety they offer. The seasons seem to establish a rhythm in our lives. How do people in Arizona or Florida know when to start or when to stop? Is it possible to have too much of a good thing? Certainly we complain about the extremes of our weather, but the valleys glorify the peaks. When an ideal day comes along, we feel it in every fiber of our being. If all we had were good days, what would we celebrate? What would we talk about?

It is the contrasts in life that give us joy. The found object is more precious because it was lost. A friend is more cherished after a separation. Silence is golden when the last guest leaves. Summer blankets our hills and fields with verigated shades of green; then autumn bursts forth in a jewel-toned spectrum of magnificent color that neither camera nor brush can capture.

These are summer's treasures. We store them in our memory to bring back to mind next winter when the cold darkness of January needs a helping hand. We must gather them quickly before the rustling leaves of autumn change summer into fall.

Winding Roads

Chapter 9

September

September 5

As the autumn air begins to nip, I am reminded of the falling leaves when I lived in a small town in Illinois. Since most of Illinois is devoted to farming and livestock, it is not noted for its trees and forests, but everyone had trees growing in their yards and around their homes as a shelter from the summer heat. The yards and the sidewalks were covered with brittle leaves that crackled under my tiny feet. Sometimes I would kick them when I walked and listen to the "swoosh."

Everyone raked leaves dutifully into several small piles. There was no such thing as leaf pick-up then. When all the leaves had been gathered together, a spot at the back of the property was designated for a bonfire that burned itself out in less than an hour. It was an autumn ritual.

Winding Roads

We enjoyed playing in a pile of leaves, much to our parents' consternation. If the pile was big enough and deep enough, we would burrow into it until we were hidden. The smaller piles we used like trampolines. Not only did this joyful sport scatter the freshly raked leaves, but we had to be brushed thoroughly before we went back into the house. Even so, we left a tacky trail as we made our way to our rooms. If the adults saw us in time, we would hear a shout from the open door, "All right now, you kids get out of those leaves!" We were frequently denied some of life's greatest pleasures by the watchful eye of parents and aunts.

We had no wooded hills where we could see the brilliant colors of autumn. Here and there throughout the town one might spot a maple tree that glowed in gold or red, but it wasn't the everyday pleasure that it is in the Northeast. However, there wasn't a kitchen in Illinois that didn't have a calendar hanging on the wall that showed pictures of these New England scenes in autumn. We couldn't imagine where these pictures came from, since we had nothing like that there. Our leaves simply turned brown, died, and were burned.

Those calendars with pictures from all over America fired our dreams and aspirations. Most of the pictures were from somewhere else, since our state was not that photogenic, so the colorful photos from far away held more allure. We stared at the California coastline and the palm trees, the Arizona desert, the steeples of New England sprouting like lilies out of a Christmas snow, or the gaily lit French Quarter of New Orleans. Once in a while they would show the Chicago skyline, or a Midwestern farm, but not very often. Chicago was the jewel in our Midwestern crown. It was about as far away as anyone went on vacation. New York City was a fantasy. These calendars opened our eyes and our mind to the fact that there was some place besides Illinois and other rivers besides the Mississippi.

The children of today are much more sophisticated and worldly. They fly to Florida to visit their grandparents or go to Disneyworld. Children accept travel as a way of life. They have been to the places we had to dream about from the pictures on our kitchen calendars.

Because of my Midwestern roots, I still find it amazing that I am living in the midst of this autumn wonderland that I couldn't imagine as a child. I will always be grateful to those calendars, because they brought the world to me before I could go to it.

September 6

My best friend Phyllis (Tag-Sale Tillie) invited me over for ice cream one warm September evening. She wanted to show me her latest sidewalk acquisitions.

Phyllis, like so many of us, has lived in the same house for over 25 years. It's full. Every shelf, every window, every tabletop is covered with "things." Most of us fall prey to knickknack bloat at one time or another.

In spite of the abundance of eye-catching objects, Phyllis and her friends go "tag sale-ing" every weekend. They come back with more adorable things, and once or twice a year, they have a sale themselves to get rid of the items they bought at other people's tag sales.

When I reached her door, she took me into the dining room where the china closet is bursting with unmatched china,

Winding Roads

Carnival glass and miscellaneous tureens, pitchers and vases. I walked past quickly for fear it might attack me.

She steered me to the small pine hutch in the corner. It must have had 47 objects on its three little shelves. These ranged from miniature Oriental opium pots to Paul Revere pewter, but the *piece de resistance* was hanging in the dining room window. It was a small beaded bird cage with a colorful little plastic parrot inside. String streamers hung from the bottom of the cage with a pebble attached to each one so that in the event of a hurricane, it would clank in the wind. It was the sort of thing one would only find at a tag sale. I'm sure it was never new.

Overwhelmed by the rush of beauty that filled the room, I couldn't keep from laughing.

"Phyllis," I sputtered, "this is wonderful. You have created a 'granny' house." I was referring, of course, to the homes of great aunts and grandparents from our childhood where the collections of a lifetime (ceramic cats, little windmills, souvenirs of Tulsa, Niagara Falls and Florida) could be discovered. How we loved to visit! My mother called these treasures "dust catchers," but we went from shelf to shelf and table to table marveling at the wonders we beheld.

Sooner or later most of us find ourselves existing in a "granny house" environment. We clutter the tables with framed pictures of the grandchildren; we display every souvenir and keepsake; we have waxed fruit, silk flowers, vases, dishes, candles and potpourri deftly crowded into whatever space we can find. We lose our focus.

In addition to this, many of us have attics and basements that are filled with the things that wouldn't fit in the living quarters. Old rugs, bird cages, Christmas cards from 1957, children's toys, our mother's china, and two generations worth of

Winding Roads

rusted tools we don't know how to use. What we accumulate on our own is bad enough, but tag sale mania inflicts the fatal wound.

I learned my lesson when my parents could no longer live in their house. They were in their late eighties, and no amount of reasoning would budge them. When they finally realized they should move, they were too fragile to move on their own. My sister and I went to St. Louis where we found an attic full of accumulation. My mother still had my father's cancelled checks, and he died when I was seven years old. They had kept every Christmas card they ever received. We found boxes of dress patterns from the 1920s and enough blankets to cover China.

In the barn we discovered chests and boxes of things my stepfather had gotten at the time of his mother's death . They had never been opened. I didn't want my children to have to go through this. I decided I would clean out my house and move from it while I was still able to handle it myself, becuase I didn't want anyone else to see what I had saved. It took me two years.When I was finished I moved into a condo with neither basement nor attic. I arrived with about one-third of what I had in the house. It was wonderful.

Now my rule is simple. If something new comes in, something old goes out. If I want to display a new picture of the grandchildren, I take an old one down. I brought with me all the things that had meaning, mainly gifts from special friends and family. The rest went. I go through my house every year and dispose of anything that is no longer necessary. That way, if I decide to move again, I'm ready.

When I started laughing, Phyllis realized she had gone too far. Instead of burying her treasures, she had buried her beautiful pine hutch beneath her treasures. You couldn't see it anymore. I picked up one of the small Chinese pots from the top shelf and said, "Phyllis, what the Sam Hill is this?"

"Clutter," She replied.

"You have three of them," I pointed out.

Phyllis called me the next day. She said she was going to sell the house and move. I assumed she was looking for something bigger so she would have room enough to expand, but she said she was going into a condo. Already she had minimized the excess on the pine hutch, and she threw the parrot in the trash. I told her that was a mistake. The parrot was the ultimate *kitsch*. It was an irreplaceable monument to bad taste. So she retrieved it. She took down a contemporary metal shelf that hung from the ceiling on the breezeway (I thought it was an old tire rim from a car that had been demolished) and hung the parrot there.

Two days later, Phyllis stopped by to show me a check for $70 she was just handed by an antique dealer. Among other things, she had sold a Victorian cruet that she bought for $4.50 for $25. Now she's considering going into business herself as "Granny House Antiques." Her bad habit is paying off.

September 15

I awoke one recent morning with a greater sense of direction than usual. My focus was on target. I knew what I wanted, and I knew what I was going to do. I'm going to retire. Enough already of agents who sit on their haunches and publishers who cannot write themselves whining about the incompetency of the average writer. No more rejection slips from editors still struggling with acne, no more exhaustive searches to

Winding Roads

find a market. Down with all the expenses that are incurred to make a sale. My writing days are over.

I was overcome by a wonderful sense of freedom. At last I would live like a "normal" person. There would be no more guilt over missed words if I wanted to go to the opera or a party. Writing was no longer my top priority. Living was.

But, I wondered, how does a "normal" person live? I have been away from it for most of my adult life. I will have to get in touch with this lifetyle again. I began by putting the kettle on the stove and making a pot of vegetable soup. It felt on track.

I will have more time for my grandchildren. I'll take them to the Bronx Zoo and the botanical gardens. We'll go to carnivals and shows. I'll teach my granddaughter how to knit and fly kites with my grandson on a balmy spring afternoon.

There will be time at last to take that boat trip across Long Island Sound from Haddam to Sag Harbor or maybe go on an eagle watch trip in the fall.

Any time I choose, I can take the day off and go to Rhode Island to walk the beaches and eat lobster rolls or wander idly into the past at Mystic Seaport. I can go to West Point for lunch or spend a few days at Annapolis when the cherry trees are dropping their pink-white blossoms like snow.

We can visit family in faraway places, my cousin in Virginia, my uncle in the Midwest, my sisters in Ohio and Las Vegas. The possibilities are endless.

Instead of writing a book, I'll have time to read a few. I can work on my genealogy, a task that has no end. I can restore my neglected doll house to a work of art. I can listen to Bach 'til I drop and go antiquing, a favorite pastime of many of my friends. I could even learn to ski. Well, maybe that's not such a good idea.

Or, if all this becomes too much, I'll sleep late, meet my friends for lunch, then dress and go to the theater at night. No point in overdoing it. That's what retirement is all about. It's only been a week, and I'm not tired of it yet.

September 23

September is house-cleaning time for many people. As I begin this annual task, I can't help but remember how little we owned when we were first married. Back in the Forties and Fifties, most girls lived with their parents until their wedding day, so they didn't have much with which to start a home of their own.

The first little one-bedroom apartment was sparsely furnished. The living room contained a sofa, a coffee table, two end tables, two lamps, and two chairs. In the bedroom there was a double bed, two night stands, a dresser, and a chest-on-chest. A table and four chairs stood alone in the dinette. The cabinets in the kitchen provided more than enough space for our dishes and pans.

We had our kitchen dishes and utensils, a matched set of Revere Ware, and, if we were lucky, several place settings of china, crystal and silver that were given as wedding gifts. Our small appliances were limited to a toaster, a waffle iron and a Mixmaster.

There weren't many frills except a few vases, bowls and figurines that also arrived as gifts. One or two pictures hung on the walls of the room, and that was about it. We knew everything we owned, and we knew exactly where it was.

Winding Roads

Over the years our possessions accumulated to department store dimensions. As our space increased, so did our "things." Along with the purchases we made ourselves, we added family treasures with the passing of grandparents, aunts and mothers. Our cabinets, closets and drawers began to bulge, a situation that was noticeably accelerated with the addition of each child.

Technology, too, played a major role in adding to the accumulation with such marvellous conveniences as, first, a blender, then a food processor, a grill, a microwave, a computer, a deep fryer, an electric skillet, a breadmaker, a pasta machine, a dehydrator, a fax machine, a cell phone, a stereo and a VCR.

Then there are the assorted items we bring back from vacation, ranging from plastic remembrances of the Cape to treasures from Italy, France and England. If, God forbid, we are "collectors" of anything from antiques to electric trains, these, too, are added to our estate. Not to be forgotten are the family pictures we have taken over the past thirty years, and the boxes of faded photographs of old, unidentified ancestors that we find in our mother's attic when she is no longer around to tell us who they are.

The bottom line is it finally gets so bad by the time we advance to middleage that we can't find anything. There is too

Technology, too, played a major role in adding to the accumulation with such marvellous conveniences as, first, a blender, then a food processor, a grill, a microwave, a computer, a deep fryer, an electric skillet, a breadmaker, a pasta machine, a dehydrator, a fax machine, a cell phone, a stereo and a VCR.

Then there are the assorted items we bring back from vacation, ranging from plastic remembrances of the Cape to treasures from Italy, France and England. If, God forbid, we are "collectors" of anything from antiques to electric trains, these, too, are added to our estate. Not to be forgotten are the family photographs of old,

Winding Roads

wonderful pictures we have taken over the past thirty years, and the boxes of faded unidentified ancestors that we find in the attic when our mother is no longer around to tell us who they are.

The bottom line is it finally gets so bad by the time we advance to middle age that we can't find anything. There is too much to remember, too much to sort out, and too many places to search. The simplest things seem to disappear; the obscure items turn up unexpectedly. Every room is filled, as are the basement, the garage, and the attic.

I have a theory that our minds work much the same way. I shudder each time I hear someone blame their age, whatever it may be, when they can't remember a name or a date. If our houses are this full of "things," think of what we have put into our heads, the people we have met, all we have learned, the places we have been, and the things we have done. We can't always find what we are looking for. Our brain is as crowded as our living rooms.

Almost everybody has rushed into the kitchen to do something important and forgotten what it was by the time they got there. The thought was crowded out by another thought. I rarely leave the house without going back three times, for my watch, my money, to fill the dog's water bowl, or to be sure I closed the windows.

With my mind swarming with ideas or deep in concentration about the day that lies ahead, I have loaded the dirty dishes into the dishwasher with the clean ones. I have on occasion forgotten where I left the dog. I have brought the mail in and gone out to get it again two hours later. My mind and my body are seldom in synch, because there is too much to think about and too much to look through.

Winding Roads

I had barely taken control of my new computer when the VCR went up in smoke, and I had to learn how to use a later model. On the heels of that came a fax and a modem. Now I am struggling with a cell phone. The input we absorb in one day is phenomenal. We're entitled to forget.

Repeating yourself is something else. This is symptomatic of age, and occurs when the input slows down, or stops completely. When we no longer are spirited by new experiences or change, we start doing replays. It's something like summer television. Forgetfulness is nothing more than an indication that we have stuffed our heads with a lifetime of living. The most absent-minded people have gained the most knowledge.

There's nothing wrong with having to check the calendar to be sure what day it is. After all, once you've retired, Thursday is just as good as Saturday, and Monday could as easily be Tuesday. It's like the silver ladle you always kept in the buffet but find in the linen closet. Who knows why you put it there? But chances are you were having an imaginary conversation with your son who wants to quit school and become a forest ranger, so you opened the first door you came to. If you still have enough recall to hack it, you may remember that you were doing things like this twenty years ago, but you didn't notice it then.

When I ran into band leader, Guy Lombrdo, three months aftrer we met, he sparkled with delight. Then he looked at me and said, "I know I'm glad to see you, but I can't remember who you are." It happens to everybody.

Winding Roads

September 26

What the world needs now are fewer psychiatrists, and more Bubbies. I'm talking about those wonderful grandmothers who came to New York via Ellis Island or who were born and rooted in the Lower East Side. They were so wise and so loving. They had solutions for which problems had not yet been discovered and a bossomy warmth that embraced anyone who passed through their portals or touched their lives. Where are they now when we need them? Their generation has fairly passed out of existence — modernized, altered and assimilated.

Almost all of them spoke Yiddish, or, if they didn't have a thorough knowledge of the language, it peppered their English with an unforgettable style. Except for the Hassidim (Orthodox Jewry) where a revival is in progress, Yiddish has become a forgotten, but never "dead," language. Those wonderful, strudel-baking, aproned Bubbeles have disappeared as well. Today's Yiddishe grandmothers use computers, drive convertibles and have their own businesses. This vital part of ethnic culture has been lost forever through assimilation and "women's lib." It breaks my heart and I'm not even Jewish.

We were reminded of all this when we saw "Crossing Delancy" recently on stage at a theater in downtown Hartford. It's about a young Jewish woman who has tried to toss off the fetters of her origins and religion by changing her style and moving uptown. She works in a book store where she meets an arrogant, self-serving author named Tyler Moss. Tyler is a wildly stereotyped "nogudnik" as drawn by the playwright. He represents everything evil in a slick, untarnished veneer. Each entry is preceded by his theme music, a strong, Wasp-like

Winding Roads

melody that describes his blond-haired, blue-eyed Adonis-like appearance in musical tones.

In spite of the young woman's pulling away from everything she is, she visits her Bubbie every Sunday. They talk. She rubs Bubbie's back, eats her strudel, and invariably the conversation comes around to Isabel's unmarried state, living in a "room," as Bubbie refers to her granddaughter's small apartment. Isabel tries to explain to Bubbie that things have changed. A woman no longer has to get married just because she's 21. She has many options. But Bubbie is unmoved. In her eyes Isabel is a lonely spinster.

Bubbie is a jewel to be treasured as the Bubbies of this world disappear. "If you want to catch a wild monkey," she tells her granddaughter, "you have to climb the tree."

Secure in who she is, Bubbie speaks of her youth. "I was the pretty one," she reminds her granddaughter with a smile of memory that glows in the past. "All the young men wanted to marry me." Then Bubbie dances the hora around the kitchen table with light-hearted glee to the tune of a Jewish melody that plays in her mind.

At this point we meet the Jewish matchmaker, Hannah. She can find someone for anyone. Isabel is no challenge. She introduces her to a nice Jewish man named Sam who owns a pickle factory. Sam is a down-to-earth, steady, reliable marriage prospect to be sure. But the match is a failure. Isabel prfers Tyler, the ultimate Wasp, until he puts the sting on her at his apartment. She gives Sam a second chance, and, with some subtle nudging from her Bubbie and Hannah, she returns to her roots.

The moral of the story is that the happiest endings find us back at our beginnings.

Winding Roads

September 28

Everywhere we look, we are surrounded by the singular, spectacular splendor of autumn in New England. Each year I am taken aback by the beauty, and each year I sit in the kitchen gazing at the sunlit colors behind my house and try once again to describe the wonder of this God-created landscape.

Like the relentless pounding of the ocean, this flow of color cannot be duplicated by man. The harshness of civilization would inflict itself upon the harmonic, tonal blend that ripples through the woods. The subtleties would be lost. Burnt orange would clash with garnet, and the gold would lose its glitter. We cannot convey this message of eternal harmony.

I find it impossible to stay in the house in autumn. The other day I went to the bank on a routine errand, and my car refused to go home. It has a mind of its own. Instead, we headed for the highway through the rolling hills of eastern Connecticut to Saybrook on the shore. I feasted on the colors like a starving man, but my appetite was insatiable. The brilliant morning sun heightened the glory of every leaf. I drove on the empty road through corridors of color.

Outside my kitchen window, a young tree that is nondescript all summer becomes a scarlet blaze in fall. Next to it is the proverbial oak, towering above the rooftop like a ruby red umbrella. Beyond that I view the copper backdrop of the forest burnished with gold and crimson. I am bathed in the beauty of my surroundings. I can enjoy the full spectrum of autumn without leaving my home. Like all good things, it comes to me if I am patient and wait.

As the leaves begin to fall, skeletons pop up amid color. They are winter's warning. Leaves of every shade flutter to the ground like whimsical ballerinas. Their graceful dance is borne on the wind as the ballet draws to a close. Dead leaves, insulating the soil against the winter snowfall, crackle and crunch beneath our footsteps. Soon a carpet of gold will cover the earth.

September 29

I feel the same burst of life in autumn that I do in spring. In fact, my year seems to begin in the fall. Everything resumes. Classes begin, theaters open, concerts start, and I am caught up in an awakening, both culturally and personally. With summer behind me, I am inspired to make a new start and enthusiastic about undertaking the accomplishments I cast aside when it was too warm and too beautiful to work. New Year's should be in the fall. The Hebrew calendar works for me. L'Chaim!

Winding Roads

Winding Roads

Chapter

10

October

October 3

The gold and crimson colors of autumn seep across the New England countryside like a wave of burnished paint that covers the hills and valleys with subtle blends of dramatic colors that scale the mountains like a symphony. There is a panoramic view around every corner. We know that God is in His Heaven, because no one could possibly plan a landscape with such perfection. Year after year, the effect is overpowering.

We took several day trips around our beautiful state this year to look at the leaves. We never tire of seeing them. One day we drove to the northwest hills to Litchfield County where there is a charming covered bridge in Cornwall still in daily use. The past is never far away in Connecticut. Along with the leaves, we

Winding Roads

enjoyed looking at the old farm houses that dot the countryside, separated one from the other by stone walls. Some of these homes have stayed in the same family for generations, but others are retreats for New Yorkers who flee the city on weekends. They are beautifully cared for and maintained.

Another day we drove south to the shore over Route 9, a lightly traveled highway that ribbons through the breathtaking beauty of the hills. We stopped at a little town called Essex on the way home where we had dinner at the old Griswold Inn. Few people outside of the immediate area have heard of Essex, one of the most charming towns in New England. It is well-known to boaters, since the Essex Island Marina is always filled, but its other tourists are mainly from within the state or across the line in Rhode Island.

Main Street is lined with quaint shops and boutiques, and the "Gris," the town's famous landmark, is at the lower end near the river. The Inn is the essence of charm year-round, and the colonial cuisine is the best. I ordered a chicken pot pie, which arrived in a large aluminum bowl, topped with a golden cloud of puff pastry that would have fed six people. Like everything on the menu, it was prepared the old-fashioned way, and the chicken was still on the bones. The simple dishes appeal to me the most, and these can still be ordered at the "Gris."

Our third trip was to that part of Connecticut that is called the "Quiet Corner." The northeast quadrant of the state is sparsely populated farmland, dotted with picturesque little towns like Coventry, Pomfret, Mansfield, and Willimantic. In Coventry we stopped at a herb farm called "Caprilands," which is open to the public. We strolled through the fading gardens that were being bedded down for winter, and I purchased Victorian Christmas cards in the gift shop.

Winding Roads

As we left Caprilands, we stopped at an old cemetery along the road to touch the past once more by reading the inscriptions on the tombstones, although many of them have been worn smooth by the elements on the unprotected hill where the cemetery is situated. Standing there by the markers of the graves of Revolutionary War soldiers, we could see for miles across the yellow-gold and scarlet countryside. Beauty is inherent in Connecticut.

One of my favorite autumnal haunts is the Catskill Mountains in New York. The colors are just as vivid there, but the majestic mountains rise like walls of gold, green, crimson and orange. One feels dwarfed and insignificant because of the overpowering presence of these massive painted mountains that form barriers on all sides of the highway. There is also a feeling of loneliness, and of awe and wonderment. It is a ponderous moment of reckoning with mortality, a reduction of self overshadowed by an unseen Being Supreme.

October 8

As the last blush of summer swept across the New England countryside, with the temperature close to 90 degrees and the leaves in brilliant color, the latest issue of a magazine to which I subscribe came in the mail, showing a large picture of the Old Man in the Red Suit on the cover, wishing me "Happy Holidays." With Halloween still three weeks away, I wasn't ready to spin into fast-forward. I tossed the magazine aside and left for the beach.

I drove down the highway through corridors of gold. The

Winding Roads

rolling hills were velvet tapestries of color. The sun reflected from every leaf. I soared like an eagle on the empty road.

When I arrived at the beach, I jumped from the car and ran to the sand. I inhaled the salt air and stood still in the summer-sun while the breeze off the water blew my cares away. Shedding my shoes, I walked across the warm sand in my bare feet. I wanted to feel the grit between my toes.

The tide was in, and the surf was active. I stopped at the water's edge and listened. The rhythmic sound of the waves lapping on the shore was the sound of life itself. I felt the heartbeat of the universe.

Gingerly I stepped into the water. I let each incoming wave lap around my legs as it slid the sand from beneath my feet. The water was cool, but not cold. The day was warm, but not hot. I smiled with joy at the simple pleasure of sand, sky and sea.

With my chair and my thermos, I sat down in the sun to watch the white caps play across the sound. My eyes followed a sail boat on the horizon. The picture was complete.

A ruffled brown sea gull, or water bird of some kind, stood on the roof of the pavilion calling loudly in my ear. He called and he called until finally another rumpled, unkempt, brown bird like himself appeared. It was easy to see why they were attracted to each other. He quickly flew down and joined her, and they walked away together, chattering up a storm.

The beach was dotted with others like myself who put responsibilities aside to take advantage of one of the last days at the shore. There were people of all ages from toddlers to retirees. The children romped and played and tested the water. The old folks put up their umbrellas and read their magazines and newspapers. All of us enjoy the seashore in our own way and at our own pace.

Winding Roads

My pace was accelerated just knowing I was alive to enjoy such a day. I didn't want to miss a single sensation. My body glowed in the warmth of the sun, and my legs tingled from the water. I heard the children laughing, the sea gulls talking, and the waves splashing as they came ashore. I saw before me a peaceful world of fulfillment.

At three o'clock the wind picked up suddenly, and it became cool. I put on my jacket. The tide was drifting out, and the day was almost over. I brushed the sand from my feet and slipped into my shoes. I gathered up my beach bag, my chair and my umbrella. I stopped at the car to take one last look before I said good-bye to summer. In one glowing day, I had reclaimed all my losses. I was alive and well, and the good earth was solid under my feet. My time had been extended; my lease had been renewed.

When I arrived home, iridescent webs streaming from the porch and the trees told the story of autumn, but I refused to think about Christmas in October. I will think about it in December. I threw out the magazine that was mostly gift hype and ads with a few articles and recipes squeezed in between. I'm living in the present, not the future. There is a time and place for everything, and certainly early October is not the beginning of the holiday season.

The miracle of living happens every day. I hope, as I go down the road, I will always remember that, and that I will use my senses to inhale the beauty of each day as it is given to me, and treasure every moment. No one is going to rob me of the present by pushing Christmas in October.

Winding Roads

October 11

If anyone ever holds a Pitiful Pets Contest, my friend Phyllis and I will win thumbs down. She has a strange little kitty that has a tail like a squirrel and spiked hair. My bug-eyed Lhasa Apso has an underbite that is so bad six lower teeth are exposed. When people visit me, no one says, "What an adorable little doggie." They don't say anything. However, she makes up for all this with a keen intelligence and affectionate disposition. She is the brightest dog I've ever owned, and I have grown to love her very much. I accept her as she is.

Phyllis, on the other hand, insists, and actually believes, that her cat is getting more beautiful as she matures, so I try to refrain from laughing when I see it. Phyllis has a good attitude toward her cat, and attitude is everything. She is certain the cat is getting prettier. Quite possibly some day it will, but in the meantime Phyllis is optimistic, and optimism is its own reward. Attitude and positive thinking control our lives, as I learned a few years ago when I went to a dermatologist about a small bump on my face.

The doctor said it would have to be removed and biopsied, since he was sure it was malignant. "Oh, no," I told him. "I'm sure it isn't. We don't get things like that in my family. We're Wasps."

Prior to the minor surgery, we had a long conference on scarring. He told me that he could not control my healing and that a scar on my face was inevitable. He was trying to protect himself from a lawsuit. "Don't worry about it," I assured him. "We don't scar. My mother wouldn't let us."

Finally, the big day arrived. The bump was removed, and three weeks later the bandage came off. The doctor was so excited

Winding Roads

I had to pull him down from the ceiling. He handed me a mirror. There was no scar. I found his excitement disarming, however, and couldn't help but wonder if I was his first success case.

"What about the biopsy?" I asked him.

"Yes," he said, "about that. The lab lost the sample. We'll never know, but I'm sure it was malignant."

"I'm sure it wasn't," I told him before I left. I don't know if my attitude helped my healing or not, but I know for certain that it didn't hurt.

October 17

When a love affair is over, far worse than losing the man of your dreams is trying to catch up on all the work you didn't do while you were otherwise occupied by romance. You open your eyes and return to reality to discover that you have become a downright slob.

The living room hasn't been vacuumed for three weeks. That's the last time he was here. There are more clothes draped on the furniture in your bedroom than there are hanging in your closet, because you couldn't decide what to wear, and there was never time to put the discards back where they belonged. You find newspapers on the dining room table that headline the Armistice, which you hope refers to Desert Storm, not World War II.

In the final three days of crisis, you forgot to feed the cats or walk the dog. There are dirty dishes in the sink and clean ones in the dishwasher that have been dry for more than a week. In the refrigerator you discover the remains of the Easter ham and

Winding Roads

two green peppers and a cucumber in the crisper floating in their own juice. There's a shriveled lemon the size of a grape, a bowl of strawberries that have fermented into wine and a chocolate Santa Claus wrapped in foil. Things are even worse than you thought.

On the desk are reminders of fifteen phone calls you never returned, and that includes three from your mother who is 89 years old. There are unanswered letters and bills to be paid, including a final notice from the electric company.

There are clothes for the cleaner and beds to be changed. The dog needs grooming, and so does the cat. The flower beds are suffering, the bushes need trimming, and the garage should be cleaned. The larder is barren, you've run out of salt, and the empty shelves in the pantry testify to the fact that you haven't eaten at home for the past six weeks, except for the night you brought in Chinese and left the cartons on the coffee table.

Yes, things are in pretty bad shape. Let's face it, he left you with a mess, and he wasn't even living here, but you were too emotionally distracted to concentrate on such ordinary things as tidying the house or doing the laundry. It took all your effort to look your best, do your nails, go to the beauty shop, raid the mall, and plan your next rendesvouz.

If there was any time left after taking care of yourself, it was spent daydreaming, creating imaginary conversations in which your wit and your charm invariably came out on top, and fantasying about steamy romantic situations that would instill new life into your diminishing love affair. Survival on the home front wasn't even a consideration. Blinded by love to the disarray, you were wired out of your wits on a lofty high that left you spinning like a top with your head in the clouds and your feet treading air in the midst of stars.

Now your broken heart is bleeding. You've lost all your

Winding Roads

hopes and expectations. Your dreams are shattered. Your world has exploded. Most of all, you feel like an idiot for having fallen for him in the first place, and especially for introducing him to your friends and family. You are kicking yourself around the block and half-way to Manhattan for your poor judgment. Your intuition warned you, but you didn't want to listen. It's hard to live with our own mistakes.

There are two things you can do at this stage of the game, or as soon as you stop crying. The first is to talk to a friend with a sense of humor and recreate the story of your doomed romance with full dramatic embellishment. Your friend will not sympathize, or offer you solace. This would be counter-productive. He (or she) will laugh at your naivete, and you yourself will see the humor in your misjudgment when you realize how silly it sounds to someone else. Once this happens, the spell is broken. You're ready to mend. Laughter is the first step to recovery.

The second thing is to remember that living clean is the best revenge. Mop the kitchen floor, put away the dishes, make the countertops sparkle and shine. Filth is depressing. Lift your spirits as you tear through the house on your Electrolux, turning chaos into order. This physical release of energy is an emotional release as well.

When you get your house under control, your life will follow. This is the natural order of things. You are in charge again. Yes, living clean is the best revenge.

October 22

I have a "roomie." It's character actress Jayne Houdyshell

Winding Roads

who has the lead in a show that is playing at one of the theaters downtown. Jayne is staying with me for the run of the show. Like so many talented people, Jayne has found steady work on the legitimate stage for the past twenty-two years, and has been performing all of her life.

It was good to sit in the kitchen and talk with a theater person again. It's been a few years since I last had this opportunity, but I have opened my doors to a number of theater people in the past. I remember one morning when I was working at Candlewood Theatre in New Fairfield, Connecticut, my husband, who was as conservative as they come, got up to go to work, and as he walked through the house to the kitchen, he saw two girls and a guy sleeping on the queen-sized sofa bed in the family room. By the time he got home that evening, they had disappeared like vapors, and he never even asked.

My fondest memory of theatrical house guests was a young man who was going to work at the theater for the summer. Through some mix-up, his dorm room wasn't ready when he arrived, and they had to put him somewhere, so they asked me if he could stay at my place just for the weekend. He looked clean enough, so I finally agreed.

It turned out he had no permanent address, so when I went to pick him up Friday afternoon, he was waiting in the lobby with everything he owned in a couple of suitcases, a backpack, an orange crate and a cage.

"Whoa!" I said. "What's in the cage?"

"My pet crabs, Sonny and Cher," he told me.

"Forget it," I said. "Let Ken take them home with him." Ken was one of our eccentric producers.

"I can't," he replied, and began trembling. "I'm afraid

Winding Roads

he'd eat them." While I saw his point, I assured him that Ken didn't know how to cook. He certainly wasn't going to shell a couple of live crabs and have them for dinner. "But my cats might," I added for emphasis.

"They'll be safe in their cage," he countered as he began tossing everything into my trunk. The orange crate, I noticed, was full of Judy Garland records which is what we played on our record players then, since there were no tapes or CD's.

"What do they eat?" I asked.

"Anything," what's-his-name told me. "A little lettuce, green things. They're vegetarians."

He brought the crabs. After I showed him his room, we put the cage on the chest in the foyer. Saturday while he was at the theater and I was writing press releases, the cats found the crabs. They reached their long feline paws between the bars of the cage and batted the seafood around until I caught them and put them outside. But I was too late. The crabs were dead. I tried to revive and excite them with a half a head of lettuce, but they didn't move.

When I picked whozis up at the theater to bring him home that night, I didn't know quite how to break the news. After all, they meant a lot to him. I wanted to be gentle.

"Eugene," I began . . .

"My name is 'Todd,'" he interrupted.

"Todd, the cats got the crabs. They're dead."

"The cats?"

"No, not the cats. Do you think a couple of vegetarian crabs are any match for two eighteen-pound cats? The crabs are dead."

"Sonny and Cher have been through a lot. They'll be all

right."

"You mean they've been pummeled by cats before?"

"They're tough."

"See for yourself," I told him as we walked through the door.

He went straight to the cage. He kneeled down next to it. I thought he was going to pray, but he began cooing at the dead crabs. "Come on, babies," he said softly. "Daddy's home. You can wake up now. Big kitties are gone. Come to daddy." They began to move. In a few minutes they were gnawing away on the head of lettuce.

Three weeks later someone went to the dorm room where Todd was staying to tell him it was time to leave for the theater, but the room was empty. He had disappeared without a trace. No one ever heard from him again.

But times have changed. Jayne came to my house *sans* cage or crate. She was a warm, wonderful person from the Midwest, and we talked theater for a couple of hours every night when she came in. I was in my element again.

October 29

Suddenly everything has changed. A gale-force wind came out of the north, and the ghost of winter appeared. Leaves fell like burnished snow. The ground was carpeted in gold, and skeletal spikes reached skyward, naked until spring. The forest looks like an x-ray. Nothing is left but the dry bones of summer.

This is the signal to convert the house for winter warmth.

Winding Roads

I get out the braided rugs for the snugness they imply, then take down the summer curtains that leave the windows open to the sunshine and the breeze. These are replaced with lace panels that form a visual barrier between us and the snow. Winter quilts and comforters in warm, dark colors are put on the beds, and the afghans are washed and scattered about where they will do the most good. The porch furniture must be stored, and, last but not least, I get out those wonderful sand-filled draft-dodgers. Cupboards and freezer are filled to keep shopping to a minimum during the bad weather. Let the cold wind blow and the snow fall when it will. I am ready.

Winding Roads

Chapter

11

November

November 2

With childlike anticipation, everyone looks forward to the first snowflakes of the season. Here in Connecticut we may see a flurry or two in November, but it is usually December before the ground is covered. The first flakes are clean, and welcome, because they signify the changing seasons that everyone who lives here enjoys. Those who don't have long since gone to Florida.

By the middle of November when the gray clouds swirl around overhead, all eyes are at the window, wondering if that magical moment has arrived. The adults are as eager as the children, but by mid-January, only the children are excited by a snowfall. Those of us who have reached the age of reason have

Winding Roads

had enough tracks in the kitchen to last us until next year, but the children never get tired of it. I was like that myself when I was little. Growing up in the Midwest, then moving to New England, I have never lived in a climate that didn't have snow.

My friends have moved to Florida in great numbers, and I'm sure a year without boots and wool scarves has acknowledged merit. Certainly the winter warmth would be conducive to good health. The rest of us have to take our chances, but apparently we are a hardy lot, since we don't seem to expire any sooner than our southern compatriots. Our immune systems have learned to fight back.

The snows of childhood are fondly remembered. We lived in St. Louis where every street was lined with two-story houses, standing straight as soldiers in a row. Most of our snows were heavy and wet since the climate was not as cold as it is here, so the moist snow clung to the trees, the overhead wires, the telephone poles and the street lamps. City snow is beautiful with its sugar-frosted houses and trees etched in crystal.

When we lived in the house in the hills in Connecticut, I can remember several full-fledged blizzards. Isolated in our homes by the gale-force winds and the swirling snow, we were nevertheless in awe of the frightening beauty of the storm. One storm lasted almost three days. When it finally stopped snowing, I opened the front door to survey the breathtakingly beautiful landscape unaware of the fact that the snow had formed a three-foot drift against the house. The snow fell in the front door, and I couldn't close it again. The drifts were over ten feet high at either end of our road, and all the private plows were commandeered by the town to clear the main thoroughfares first, so we were cut off from the world for two more days, waiting for the secondary roads to be plowed, so that we might be rescued from the savage

Winding Roads

storm that held us hostage.

Autumn is spent, like last week's paycheck. The colors are gone, the clocks have been set back, and the Dark Ages are ready to begin in earnest. Skeletal trees are silhouetted against a sombre sky. The highways are clogged with the "snow birds" heading for Florida, dragging their big metal "nests" behind them, while we who stay behind dip deep into our reservoir of optimism as we surmount this period between an amber autumn and a pastel spring.

November 3

A rainy day is a welcome sight in November. It gives us a chance, and an excuse, to stay indoors and tackle some of the tasks, both pleasant and loathsome, that we have been putting off for several months when the call of the outdoors was more than we could resist. There is a great satisfaction in getting these things done.

I believe it was Fibber McGee of old radio fame who had a box or jar where he wrote down all his rainy-day chores on little pieces of paper. When the time was right, he extracted one from the jar and did it. That's not a bad idea, but we should have two jars, one marked "Pleasant," the other "Loathsome." That way, we could alternate between the two. Otherwise we might draw three "loathsomes" in a row and give up altogether. I'm going to try it this winter.

In my "pleasant" jar I will put "Sort through four crates of old photos." Everyone has these, neatly stacked in an attic or closet. I have more than my share, as I now have all of my mother's old photos along with my own. This winter I am going to go through these boxes. It's a wonderful long-range pastime for rainy days and could very well carry me through until spring.

Also in my "pleasant" jar I will place "Finish the rug I have been hooking for four years." Right on its heels will come "Finish the rug I have been hooking for two years." I'm a great starter, but before I can finish one thing, something better comes along. This winter I am going to complete some of these past-due, partly-done projects.

In my "loathsome" jar I will make a note to turn one of my doll houses into a log cabin. Working on the doll house is a tiresome task because it isn't anything you can rush. First, the strips of wood must be measured and cut. Accuracy is important, or you could seal up a window. Then they must be stained before they can be glued into place. Staining requires a couple of coats, and lacquer on top. Each one has to dry. Added to this is the problem of where to put all the cut strips of wood while you're working on them, and how to remember which strip goes where. Then they must be glued to the structure so perfectly that they will fit between each other at both ends of the building to give the log effect. If I survive the "logging" of the house, I then have to cover the roof with cedar shingles. Yes, this definitely goes under "loathsome" even though the end result may be quite pleasant.

Other pleasant tasks that I will work on are completing the family history on my father's side. This is both pleasant and loathsome, because it requires a lot of backtracking, looking up, verifying, and research, so I shall withhold judgment.

In the pleasant category I have stacks of magazines that I haven't had time to look at, and to which I finally quit subscribing when I discovered they are more or less the same from one year to the next. In addition to the magazines, there are always books I want to read when I can find the time.

Winding Roads

Rainy days are marvellous for writing letters or baking cookies, provided you can resist eating them as fast as they come from the oven. When I bake cookies, I put them into tins as soon as they cool, and freeze them. The purpose of this is so I won't eat them, but I have discovered that frozen cookies aren't that bad. The can in the freezer empties quickly. If someone drops by who isn't into popping frozen cookies, I quickly throw them into the microwave.

The frigid, blustery days that extend from Thanksgiving until mid-March are ideal for doing all the things that good weather prevents the rest of the year. Snow days have their merit.

On the other hand, maybe I will put the jars into the closet, along with the unfinished rugs and sweaters and the boxes of old photos, and go to Florida for a month or two. It will all be here when I get back.

November 8

Once my teenagers left home to go to college, and I stopped working in theater, I fell behind the times. I no longer knew what was "in" or what was "out." When my recent theatrical house guest arrived for a two-month visit, I was still wearing saddle oxfords and knee socks, listening to Guy Lombardo records on an outdated stereo. It was pathetic.

Jayne showed up carrying her own food, and each evening when she came in, I was fascinated watching her eat a number of dishes I had never heard of, mostly Italian. I had just learned how to order from a French menu, and I was outdated already. Italian had taken over. Since I am allergic to oregano, this is of little interest to me. However, I didn't want to be left behind, so Jayne brought me up to this century.

The trendy people are drinking latte and capuchino, frequently served with biscotti, a Mediterranean dog biscuit-type thing that is best dunked into the aforementioned beverages.

Cajun or blackened anything is trendy, as are portobello mushrooms and polenta. Likewise, anything with the word "penne" in it is apparently very satisfying to today's appetite for inexpensive Italian dishes. After all, how much does it cost to boil a pot of noodles?

Garlic mashed potatoes are a new addition to the trendy menu, as are sun-dried tomatoes, bagels and barbecue.

Creme Brulee is a favored dessert, but both old-fashioned bread pudding and meatloaf are on the comeback trail.

Many items that were trendy are no longer on the list. These include French delicacies such as quiche, croissants, fondue and crepes. We have also seen the passage of onion dip, spinach dip, soul food and comfort food, popular items that no party was complete without a few years ago. I still like them but don't admit to it in mixed company.

Then we come to the foods that are as far down on the list as they can get. These are items that are no longer trendy and can only be eaten in secret. Heading the parade, of course, is tuna and noodle casserole. Then we have pot roast, chicken and dumplings, egg salad, tomato surprise and cabbage. There are many others. If your mother fixed it, chances are it's out of favor now.

While French food has been replaced by Italian, and Chinese is always there, where will our next fad foods come from? I suspect the Middle East. I think seedy things will replace some of the harsh Italian seasonings. Foreshadowing is beginning to appear on our menus, subtly testing the waters. I'm all for camel steaks and sesame seeds, provided they don't contain oregano.

November 14

My ancestors didn't arrive on the Mayflower, but my fifth great-grandfather, Simon Linder, came to America from Germany in 1733. A large number of refugees came to this country from Germany and Great Britain as indentured servants. This slave trade was carried on by unscrupulous sea captains who sailed from the ports of Europe and England.

Caravans of gaily colored wagons, drawn by well-matched horses traveled the German countryside. As soon as a crowd would gather in the small towns along the way, a man would appear on one of the wagons, singing the praises of America where "the streets are paved with gold, and everyone is rich." He offered free passage to anyone who wanted to go. The "free" passage would be paid for at the end of the trip when the passengers were sold before they could leave the ship.

These "recruiters" were called "Newlanders," and they were not popular with the German government. In fact, they were banned from certain areas of the country, since the Newlander's job was to lure the unhappy peasants to the port for the benefit of the sea captains, thus reducing the beleaguered population even further. If the captain could not fill his ship with volunteers, the quota was reached by kidnapping men off the streets or from the taverns near the wharf.

It was not unusual for wayfarers headed toward a port

Winding Roads

to meet people returning to the homes they had just left in Germany, because the shipmasters had raised the fare, and they could no longer afford to make the crossing. Some of those who did not have the money accepted the captain's offer for a "free" trip; others returned to Germany rather than risk what lay ahead.

When Simon, his wife and five children arrived in Rotterdam, he went to the dock to try to book passage. There were three ships in port preparing to set sail for the New World, but two of these would not accept paying passengers. They would take only those who would turn a profit at the end of the trip. The Linders crossed on the third ship, since they were able to afford the fare.

Their crossing took three months. When they arrived in Philadelphia, a doctor came on board, as everyone had to be examined for a number of contagious diseases. Following this, the men were taken to City Hall where they had to sign an oath of allegiance to King George II. After that they were free to collect their families from the ship and proceed toward their destination.

However, when the other two ships that carried the refugees arrived, the passengers were half starved, since they had not been provided with enough food, and what they had was spoiled. Disease was rampant, and as many as one-third of the passengers died at sea and were tossed overboard. Other reports that have survived to the present day tell of people actually starving to death on these trips when their daily rations were cut to a cup of water and a slice of bread. Men caught trying to steal food for themselves or their families were taken on deck and beaten until the blood ran down their bare backs. Sanitary conditions were non-existent.

When these ships pulled into the harbor, everyone was

examined by the doctor out in the open. The men were then marched like prisoners to City Hall to sign the oath of allegiance. After that, they had to return to the ship, and no one could leave until sold. The young single people were the first to go, the elderly the last. Families were separated, and the term of service was anywhere from three to seven years, at which time a man was given a suit of clothes and a horse, and a woman got a dress and sometimes a cow.

This is how a great number of our forefathers began their lives in America, but still it was better than their lot in Europe, because here at least they had hope, something that was denied them by the crowned heads of Europe.

November 24

The First Thanksgiving Proclamation came out on June 20, 1678, fifty-eight years after the Pilgrims arrived in Plymouth. It did not include gluttony, but called for a day to be set aside for prayer and fasting in thanks for their survival to establish what had by then become an almost thriving community.

What we actually celebrate is that first-year feast that was held after the harvest of 1621, calling it "Thanksgiving" and moving it to November to coincide more closely to the month of their first settlement on America's shores. By the time they held this feast, there were only seven women left to cook it. The rest had lost their lives during the course of the winter, buried at night in unmarked graves.

They had spent a difficult year trying to survive in this new world, the "land of plenty." It did not live up to its hype,

Winding Roads

since they had a hard time finding enough food to endure. They subsisted mainly on what was left over from the trip and whatever they could shoot. They weren't very good at this, since they didn't have to kill what they ate in England or Holland.

Things got so bad they sometimes ate their plates. Since serving dishes were in short supply, two people frequently shared a "trencher," the wooden bowls from which they ate, but sometimes there were not enough of these, so the meal would be served on a slice of hard bread to be used as a plate. By the time the warm food soaked into the stale bread, it became palatable, so they ate that, too. This custom was carried over from medieval times in Europe.

The Pilgrims did not think of themselves as "Americans," because the country hadn't been created yet. They were "English." This was their culture, and to maintain their ties with England, they brought with them to the new country such things as rye and other English grains, but the English seeds did poorly in the American soil. Their crops failed.

They were not vegetable eaters, but during the hardships of that first winter, they were happy to eat whatever they could find, even sweet potatoes. They ate anything that was edible and a few things that were not. They spent most of their time foraging for food, as they tried to use what little strength they could muster to build their houses and take care of the sick. Food was a primary problem, and they were always hungry. You didn't see any fat Pilgrims.

Then Squanto, the good Indian, came along and taught them how to plant corn, how to use it, and how to eat it. When the English crops failed, they still had a fine supply of corn, so they decided to hold a feast to celebrate their surviving that first,

Winding Roads

long, hard winter in New England.

The children gathered shellfish from the streams and seashore and wild greens from the woods. The men, who were finally learning to shoot, went out and brought back turkeys, ducks and geese. In addition to this, they had fresh fruits and dried, corn in a number of forms, and wine made from the grapes.

While the Indians had been invited to the feast, the Pilgrims did not expect Chief Massasoit to arrive with ninety of his braves! They didn't have enough food for these additional guests. When one of the English muckety-mucks, probably Gov. Bradford himself, explained the embarrassing situation, the Chief understood, and sent his braves out with their bows and arrows. They returned with five deer, venison enough for everybody. The feast lasted for three days.

The traditional Thanksgiving meal that we celebrate today is not too far removed from that first feast in 1621, with one major exception, maybe two. The turkey and fowl had no stuffing. This was added later by some inventive cook. Also, the bread on the table was probably corn bread, and dessert was Indian pudding, not pumpkin pie. It is concluded by historians that this celebration was held in the summer, since the poor Pilgrims did not have a building big enough to hold this many people in cold weather, so it is unlikely that pumpkins were available at this time of year. Cranberries, sweet potatoes, squash and succotash were safe bets as side dishes. And if you want to get really traditional, forget the matched china, and serve it all on a slice of stale bread.

We rarely think about how these early Pilgrims got here, or how they lived. One hundred and two Pilgrim passengers made the trip across the Atlantic on the 106-foot *Mayflower*. They were berthed in the dark, windowless "'tween decks," quartered in small curtained cabins or bunks along the sides of the ship around a common area that served as a dining room, kitchen, and laundry. The Pilgrims had to subsist for sixty-six days on the food and stores they had brought with them. One baby was born at sea, and two adult lives were lost during the crossing.

When they landed on American soil, they hastily built small one-room cabins that were dirt-floored and dark. They had no windows. Furnishings were scant. Provisions were kept in the dry overhead lofts, but the family slept on straw mattresses on the damp floor. Cooking was done over an open fire. It is hard to imagine how anyone survived at all. At this point in time it is difficult, if not impossible, to relate to the hardships and deprivations the founders of our country endured as they blazed the first path through the forests that would bring us where we are today. We take too much for granted.

The meaning of Thanksgiving, like that of Christmas, has been diluted by commercialism and the great American pursuits such as football, television, and parades. To many, Thanksgiving means little more than the beginning of heavy-duty shopping for Christmas.

Each of us should take time, silently, if not out loud, around the turkey table, to give our thanks and think about all we have for which we should be thankful. We need to get back to "meanings."

Certainly Thanksgiving is a time of homecoming. Children and grandchildren crowd into our homes. Lights emanate from every window of our houses. We are warm, we are well-fed, and adequately clothed.

This year, as we go around the table offering our own personal thanks, I will lead the parade. I am thankful, not only for all I have, which is far less than many people, but I am especially thankful just to be here, to be healthy and well. And I am thankful to those Pilgrims who made the day possible.

The first Thanksgiving feast lasted for three days. Mine will only last for one afternoon, but it will take me three days to get it on the table! I don't mind. I am glad I am able to do it and to share it with those I love and who love me in return.

November 26

At one time or another it happens to all of us. Somebody does it to us, and we want to do it back to them. We want to "get even." We seek revenge, only in its highest form, of course. We certainly don't want to start a war or anything like that, but we want the last word. We want to teach that person a lesson.

The act of dishonor may come from a slight by a relative we never liked in the first place. It can happen in the office when somebody walks on our face climbing up the ladder to the top. It can stem from malicious gossip that tarnishes our character. Certainly it frequently comes from an ex-husband, an ex-husband's new wife, or a boy friend on his way out. Whatever it is, and whoever does it, it hurts our ego and our feelings. We feel honor-bound to do something about it.

When this happens, the first thing to remember is do nothing for twenty-four hours. Wait for the dust to settle. Our first reaction to such a misdeed is invariably volatile. Violence

Winding Roads

solves nothing. We cannot slash our neighbor's tires, or toss a Molotov cocktail through an ex-husband's picture window. These things are illegal. We must find a way to stay within the confines of the law, and still soothe our ego that has been bruised by this rejection.

Therefore, we may spend the 24-hour cool-off period contemplating the worst possible retaliation, but it's amazing what a good night's sleep will do. We see things differently in the morning. We begin to rationalize, and our revenge becomes somewhat less violent, although probably just as damaging.

Let's face it, if we exchange malice for malice, there is no telling where it will end. Hurt feelings are slow to heal, and a bruised ego is even slower. The whole thing could escalate into a small war. You did it to me, I do it to you, you do it back to me, I do it back to you, etc. This is not the way to go, because it can become such a thorn in our sides that we can no longer function efficiently. It takes too much energy to plan the next attack or ward off the last one.

My suggestion is, instead of doing something rotten to the person who did it to you, do something nice for yourself. This can be whatever you can afford. If you have the wherewithal to take a cruise or buy a new car, go for it. Most of us can't afford to be that lavish, so we settle for less, a box of candy, a dozen pink roses, or a Cashmere sweater. Whatever your gift to yourself, it will take your mind off of the negative aspect of the situation, while you concentrate on the pleasurable positive. It works. You will feel better immediately, without hurting anyone else, which, in the long-run, never makes us feel good. The barbs are certainly much easier to take in a new Mercedes or designer sweater.

However, if you want to achieve the ultimate revenge, go out and get something for yourself that that person always

Winding Roads

wanted. It doesn't get any better than this.

November 28

Our first snow cover came last night after most people had gone to bed. I turned out the lights in the living room, and watched the king-sized flakes floating silently past the street light, entranced as always by the broken ribbons that drift from the sky to cover the earth with a soft, satin blanket. Finally, at midnight I went to bed, feeling snug and content in the warmth of my room.

Winding Roads

Chapter

12

December

December 9

Every December just before Advent, there used to be a Novena at the old Rock Church in North St. Louis. I wasn't Catholic, but most of my friends were, so I went with them. They were praying for husbands. The Novena was nine straight days of prescribed prayers with the assurance that these prayers would be answered. Whatever was asked would be given. It sounded like a good deal to me. Guaranteed delivery.

In the church I attended with my family, one did not pray for specific things, like a sled, or a job, or a husband. We prayed for the sick, or for spiritual success, or to wipe out all evil. Since the sick inevitably died anyway, and evil persisted throughout the world, I had little faith in prayers, but it was different for Catholics. Whatever they prayed for, they received, and they never doubted the outcome. This kind of faith was new to me.

We went to Novena services straight from work. The streetcar emptied at the church. It drew people from all over the city. Apparently everyone knew of the miracles that a Rock Church Novena could inspire. There was a feeling of joyful anticipation as we entered the church and sat down. By the time the Novena began at 5:30, it was standing room only. The pews were filled to capacity. The weather had turned cold, and as latecomers walked down the aisle, they blessed everyone with the incense of the crisp outside air that clung to their clothes. It was like smelling laundry right off the line.

The service was in Latin, but my friends made all the appropriate responses. I was spellbound by their fluency. The songs were in Latin as well, songs like "Tantum Ergo," and "Oh, Maria." Soon it no longer seemed like a foreign tongue, but rather a mysterious language out of the past that belonged to the mystical events that would take place here.

When I looked around, I saw people present who were lame or afflicted, no doubt praying for a cure. There were old people, and young, but the majority of the participants were working girls like my friends and myself. Were they all praying for husbands, I wondered. Since I wasn't Catholic, I figured I was disqualified, so I didn't pray for anything, but studied instead the devout faces in the pews.

Women were not allowed to enter the church bareheaded, so before we went in, I put a square of black lace on my head that one of my friends had loaned me. I felt like a Catholic. I liked being a part of the mystery. The inside of the church was warm and beautiful. The pomp and the ceremony created an environment of virtuous beauty and cleansed the

Winding Roads

mind of worldly matters that had no place in the spirituality of the church. I surrendered to my surroundings. I read the Latin responses with everyone else, and I received the Gift of Peace.

Only a few Catholic churches hold Novenas any more. Young ladies no longer pray for husbands.

December 11

Here in New England, we have to prepare for winter. The farther out in the country we live, the more we must do to get ready.

As we look forward to the first snow, we anticipate the worst possible disaster. Remembering ice storms of the past that left some of us without power, heat and water for almost a week, we are as busy as squirrels burrowing in for the winter. We hurry up and wait.

The gardens are put to bed, and the spring bulbs are in the ground. The wrought-iron furniture is tucked away. Patios and porches are bare and ghostly as outdoor laughter is sealed into storage. The leaves are raked, and the gutters are cleaned. Each little house becomes an island, a snug harbor of warmth and protection.

For those with wood-burning stoves and fireplaces, it means making certain that a supply of logs is conveniently stacked near the door. Driveways are staked for the snow plow. At last the outdoors stands ready. The world, as we know it, will soon hibernate and sleep like a bear beneath a cover of snow.

Inside the house, people used to change curtains, slipcovers and rugs with the seasons, but this is less likely now with central heat and air conditioning since our temperatures stay constant throughout the year. There was a time, however, when the warm, braided rugs of winter came up in the spring so that bare feet could draw the coolness from the boarded floor in summer. Heavy drapes designed to keep out the drafts were taken down to allow the breeze to billow and blow the diaphanous panels that were left there. Many families kept two sets of bed spreads and slip covers to change the look and the feel of the house with the weather. These were different times, indeed.

We check and replace the batteries in the lantern, the flashlight, the radio and the hand-held television. We leave a candle and matches in every room and fill the kerosene lamps. Extra blankets are on standby, and afghans adorn the sofas. We stock the pantry with powdered milk and canned food that requires no preparation, remembering to keep the old can opener handy.

Once all this is done, we are ready to snuggle up next to the fire or the cat, as the case may be, and enjoy the season that challenges and stirs our pioneer instincts. We are prepared for nature's fury, secure in the knowledge that we can survive until the work crews restore the power, or the snow plow digs us out from under.

Most of us who live here find a certain excitement in the mysterious harshness of the seasons. We thrive on the contrasts. Dyed-in-the-wool New Englanders cannot be lured away by a year of nothing but sunshine. We like it the way it is. The beauty of a fresh snow offsets its inconvenience. It is an exciting obligato to the tune of our sandy beaches in summer.

Seldom do we need the emergency measures we have

Winding Roads

taken, but there is a great satisfaction in being prepared "just in case." The bad-weather days are a good excuse to break routine and stay in. Cancellations are a reprieve. The soup kettle goes on, and the cocoa comes out as busy schedules are interrupted by snow and sleet. We find time to enjoy the winter, bearing in mind that it is, after all, nothing more than the harbinger of spring.

December 14

When I was a little girl, I had three great aunts, Aunt Minnie, Aunt Mae and Aunt Maude. They were old ladies who pattered around the house in felt slippers and lisle stockings rolled below their veiny, knobby knees. They lived together with Aunt Minnie's husband, Uncle Andy. Uncle Andy looked like a barrel-chested troll. He had a booming voice and bushy gray eyebrows that moved up and down when he talked. He didn't like children, so we tried to keep out of his way.

Aunt Minnie was a large woman with misplaced breasts that swung below the place where her waist used to be. However, her good nature and laughing disposition overcame her structural flaws. She was my favorite great aunt.

Aunt Mae was a mystery. She was there, taking up space, but like a ghost, she had no identity. Her presence was not felt. She moved about the room, pouring coffee and clearing the table, but she never had an opinion.

Aunt Maude was the most interesting of the three. She was a tall, skinny lady with a homely face, but that was all right, because she had other attributes. She was psychic. She told fortunes with cards and made tables move in dimly lit rooms.

Winding Roads

We always visited the great aunts the Saturday before Christmas. When we arrived at the house, I rang the bell three times. This was the signal that told them that family had come for a call. Aunt Minnie opened the door, effusive and laughing.

"Come in, come in," Aunt Minnie said, as she hustled everyone through the door to the warmth inside. Uncle Andy was standing in the hall, his gun drawn. Uncle Andy always answered the door with a gun in his hand. We were lucky Aunt Minnie got there first. I don't know who Uncle Andy was expecting, but I have since wondered what business he was in.

"Grmmmfft," he said with a half-smile, shoving the gun into his belt. "Yiirt frrjppt," he continued. His voice seemed to emanate from his eyebrows, and I could never understand what he was saying. Maybe he was talking troll.

"The same to you, Uncle Andy," I replied. I figured that was safe.

"Come on in the kitchen. The coffee's hot," Aunt Minnie invited. Aunt Maude and Aunt Mae were already there. Aunt Minnie handed each of us kids a small cedar box of hard candy. The yellow streaked wood was like satin, and when the lid was raised, the fragrance of cedar filled our heads. Next to vanilla, it was our favorite smell. We went into the living room to join our cousins who were already there.

"Grmmmmft jygpfftml . . . " Uncle Andy called after us as we left. He was friendlier than usual.

In a few minutes everyone came into the room where we were sitting. "I had a box like that when I was a little girl," Aunt Maude said.

"Yours was bigger, Maude. You kept doll clothes in it," my grandmother said to her sister. "I kept handkerchieves in mine." This set off a volley of recollections of childhood among the great aunts and my grandmother. I couldn't believe that the great aunts were ever younger than they were then. I thought everyone was the age they were when they came into my life, and I expected them to stay that way. Anything that happened before did not exist.

I tried to imagine Aunt Minnie as a bride, or Uncle Andy as a young man, exchanging their troll-like vows under a bridge. I looked at Aunt Mae, but nowhere could I find the little girl who ran through the woods and gathered berries. Aunt Maude couldn't possibly have been a willowy young woman waltzing around the dance floor in her wide-sashed dress, her golden blonde ringlets piled high on her head. The mystery of their past lives was more than I could fathom.

I wondered if all old people were young at one time. If so, where did it go, this youth they describe? Would I grow old, too? I couldn't wait to grow up so I could wear lipstick and high-heeled shoes, but some day would I be as old and wrinkled as the great aunts? No, I decided, it couldn't happen to me. I refused to part with my youth. I was certain that I had an immunity against aging.

I was wrong.

December 18

There is nothing quite like the beauty or the excitement of Christmas in the city. It has a festive quality that the Christmas card artists rarely sketch. Apparently they think Christmas only comes in the country where smoke curls from the chimneys of old farm houses nestled in snow-covered hills and the Christmas trees are decorated with cranberries and popcorn.

The enchanting displays in the department store windows were one of the city's stellar attractions. My mother took me downtown every year to see these awesome displays. These fanciful windows featured colorful scenes of Christmas with mechanical people moving about their duties, doing the same things over and over again.

There was Santa's workshop where the little mechanical elves were busily putting toys together for delivery on Christmas Eve. They hammered and stitched, packed and pounded.

Another window showed Grandma's house where she was in the kitchen preparing the Christmas goose while Grandpa snoozed in a chair, never awakening from his mechanical dream.

There were scenes from fairy tales and favorite stories, and always a train in one of the windows that climbed precipitous mountains of fluffy white snow, then disappeared into a long tunnel, emerging at the other end with all its lights aglow. Children, bundled up in their scarves and mittens, stood entranced before each window until their mothers pulled them away with the promise of something better still to come. These windows were among the greatest joys of childhood, as any kid who lived in the city knows.

Christmas was everywhere. There were Santa Clauses ringing bells on all the street corners, and traditional Christmas carols were piped throughout the stores. As the day drew closer, carolers appeared in public places, standing next to towering trees hung with fragile glass ornaments, dripping with silver tinsel and smelling of pine. There were trees in all the hotel lobbies, in the office buildings, restaurants and stores.

The snow in St. Louis was heavy and wet. It clung to the

Winding Roads

trees and overhead wires. Every building, every tree, everything in this city-world looked as if it were outlined with sugar frosting. When the sun came out, rows of icicles edged the frosted roofs, making them look like gingerbread houses in a Hansel and Gretel world. Sleds came up from basements, and small skis appeared under Christmas trees. Children put on the skis and slid down miniature hills as happy and fulfilled as if they were in the Alps.

The city bustled with excitement at Christmas. The stores were crowded with happy shoppers. The air was filled with music and bells. The abundance of life made Christmas a time of excess. Store windows each year surpassed the beauty of the windows the year before. The fragrance of city foods escaped from the houses and the baker's. There was an explosion of good cheer, boxed chocolates, and poinsettias, and every vacant lot was filled with freshly cut trees exuding the sharp-sweet fragrance of pine.

Christmas in the city was lavish. The city was wrapped in gaily strung lights and festooned with tinsel in silver and gold, but when the bells rang at midnight to announce the birth of Christ, the city fell silent in praise.

December 21

As every parent knows, there is no sorrow in the empty nest. It never lasts that long. They keep coming back, and each time they return there are more of them.

My son was married in June two weeks after he and his bride graduated from UConn. We heaved a sigh of relief. With

Winding Roads

our other son in the Navy for the next nine years, the house was empty.

A week later Larry and his wife returned from their honeymoon. since he was leaving for grad school in Vermont in September (our treat, of course), they decided it would be silly to rent a place for a couple of months while they worked at Chuck's Steak House as a well-educated cook and an actuarial waitress. They'd stay with us.

It didn't matter. It would give them a chance to save a little money, since there is no such thing as room or board at mommy's house. I was never home anyway. I was working an eighteen-hour day seven days a week at the theater, and they worked nights at Chuck's, so we hardly saw them, except at meals.

In September we waved good-bye to their van with its trailer full of wedding gifts. Now at last I could start working on my dream for a champagne-colored house. Enough of the dark, drab colors that would absorb childhood fingerprints and peanut butter. *Architectural Digest* was my destiny!

The decorators began the mass overhaul. Walls, furniture and carpet were all champagne. The empty nest was a showcase by the time Larry and his wife came home for Christmas. I had invited them for the weekend, but when they arrived, he told us they could stay a week. What he didn't tell us was that they had a hunting dog.

As they opened the door, this brown and white monstrosity came bounding through the house, ran into the living room and raised his leg at the artificial tree I had just finished decorating, spotting and staining the brand new one-week-old champagne carpet. My mind went blank.

Winding Roads

It was a critical moment in my relationship with my son. If I blew up like I wanted to, it could seriously and permanently damage our ideal mother-and-son relationship, a situation I had never firmly defined, but suspected might be present. I stayed calm, and watched my son go to pieces. It was one of the highlights of my life.

When I didn't raise my voice, he fell apart. He was embarrassed and suffering. It was my victory all the way. He ran to the kitchen to get some rags to clean the rug, all the time apologizing profusely. I, in the meantime, was contemplating the joy of having this beast around for a week, not my son, the dog. I don't remember its name. I don't even remember its gender.

"I can't understand it," my son said. "He's never done anything like that at home." Then, turning to the dog, he reprimanded., "Bad dog! Bad dog!"

The dog, in an effort to atone for his stupidity and ill manners, decided to do the only thing he was trained for. He posed in the perfect point like a gaggle of geese were flying through the dining room. He stood there poised awaiting praise and rewards, but unfortunately the dog, penitent though he was, was "pointing" down the hall at the dirty clothes hamper. It was a moment to be reckoned with.

"Don't worry about it, darling," I said to my son, so calm he wanted to run outside and check the address to be sure he had the right house. "Those things happen. I'd be more concerned about a hunting dog that can't tell a plastic Christmas tree from a forest, and who points at a hamper full of dirty laundry. We're lucky he didn't retrieve a sock."

"Bad dog! Bad dog!" my son kept saying, as if the dog cared. He had the vocabulary of an insect. Nothing registered.

Winding Roads

When my son finished scrubbing the brand new champagne carpet that was still fuzzing, he said, "I'm sorry, mom. Next time we'll leave him at the kennel."

"Fine," I responded with a smile that would make Whistler's mother look like a hooker. "I'll pay for it."

December 24

As a teenager, I used to go caroling every year with a group from our church, collecting money for the Tuberculosis Society. We only went where the money was. Our group was sent to solicit the tall apartment-hotels in the West End of St. Louis and the large homes of the wealthy people who lived there. We caroled on Christmas Eve when giving was at its peak and generosity overflowed. The Tuberculosis Society loved us, and the disease was brought under control, thanks in part to our persistent singing.

The large apartment houses presented no problem, as it was warm inside the halls. We climbed up floor by floor, then rode the elevator down. Foolishly, we did the apartments first and were nipped by the cold when we walked from mansion to mansion.

Once the people at one of the big houses invited us in for hot chocolate. All nine of us stepped gingerly out of our world and into theirs.

The reception hall had marble floors, wood paneled walls, and a golden oak staircase leading to the rooms above. The man who let us in was wearing a black suit with a white shirt and black bow tie. He looked like Fred Astaire, but he wasn't dancing.

Winding Roads

He walked with a stately gait as he led us into the drawing room where several other people were gathered. All the men were in black suits, and the women had on floor-length evening gowns that shimmered when they walked. They were drinking Champagne.

At one end of the room was a Christmas tree that reached to the ceiling and filled the bay window in the front of the house. At the other end was a grand piano. A man was seated at the keyboard, his fingers rippling idly over the keys.

"Let's all sing carols together," one of the beautiful ladies suggested.

"Yes, let's," a fat woman agreed. We walked across the room to the piano, and everyone began to sing "O, Little Town of Bethlehem." Their voices were magnificent. I stopped singing and listened. I wanted to absorb every detail of the moment, from the paintings on the wall to the quiet, gentle joy that filled the room. I wanted to remember that Christmas Eve the rest of my life.

We sang a couple more carols before a maid in a starched white apron brought us a tray of hot chocolate and cookies. When we had been served, we gathered around the fireplace where pine-scented logs snapped and crackled as they burst into brilliant orange flame. While we were drinking our cocoa, the fat lady walked over to the piano and sang "O Holy Night." The familiar carol was encapsuled in gold by her 24-carat voice.

When the song was finished, the lady with the beautiful voice stood with one hand resting on the piano, and she didn't look fat any more. Her flawless, soprano voice made her beautiful. She acknowledged the applause by bowing her head

Winding Roads

gracefully. Two of the men shouted "Bravo!" and their host handed her a crystal vase filled with pale pink roses. Everyone laughed at the joke. I hoped she would sing another carol, but it became clear that it was time for us to leave. The fat lady had sung. It was over.

As we prepared to go, the men got out their wallets and put money into our collection can. We thanked them profusely for their hospitality and their gift. As soon as we were out of sight of the house, we opened the canister to see how much they had given. The Tuberculosis Society was eighteen dollars richer, a remarkable sum in 1939. And we had been enriched by the Christmas Eve joy we had shared with strangers who welcomed us into their home, spreading the love and peace of Christmas through the magic of song and friendship.

December 25

Charlie Brown, in his annual Christmas show, is found struggling with the meaning of Christmas. While all his friends are happy and singing tuneful songs of the season, Charlie Brown is moping. Not even the prize-winning lights and paper chains on Snoopy's dog house can mollify him. If anything, the artificiality only makes him feel worse. He is completely put off by the commercial aspects of the holiday. He cannot get through the glitter to uncover the real meaning of Christmas.

Finally, it is Linus (who has donated his precious "blankee" to be used as a Christmas tree skirt) who shows Charlie Brown what it's all about. Taking center stage, he gives a soft,

Winding Roads

gentle reading from the Bible for Charlie Brown who is standing in the wings.

> "And, lo, the angel of the Lord came upon them, and the glory of the Lord shone round about them; and they were sore afraid.
>
> And the angel said unto them, Fear not; for, behold, I bring you good tidings of great joy, which shall be to all people.
>
> For unto you is born this day in the city of David a Saviour, which is Christ the Lord.
>
> And this shall be a sign unto you: Ye shall find the babe wrapped in swaddling clothes, lying in a manger.
>
> And suddenly there was with the angel a multitude of the heavenly host praising God, and saying,
>
> 'Glory to God in the highest, and on earth peace, good will toward men.'"

Occasionally, all of us, like Charlie Brown, need to be reminded of the true meaning of Christmas. The beautiful story of the birth of Christ is set forth simply in the old King James Bible in the second chapter of Luke. If we read this story and sing the carols of Christmas that praise the birth of the Lord, we will experience again the undiluted, childhood joy of Christmas.

Winding Roads

December 29

The day is cloudy and gray. The snow has been falling since dawn. Its unblemished beauty spreads across the yards in silver silence. Like a velvet shawl, it enfolds the land and the rooftops while I doze gently in my chair. There is no sound or human contact to disturb my nap. No one can reach me to interrupt my reverie or invade my snuggly, silent world. I am alone with my dreams.

When I awaken, I am seduced by the lure of the kitchen. This only happens on snow-bound days. Soon the smell of brown sugar and freshly baked cookies crowds the rooms with joy, reaching into every corner of my childhood. For a moment I am caught in the snows of yesterday when I was the child, and "she" was the mother. With a cup of warm cocoa, I sample a cookie straight from the oven, and I am eight years old again.

Neither the dog nor the cats will venture out on a day such as this, until the necessity becomes so great that they have no other choice. The old cats are semi-comatose all winter. They hibernate like bears, interrupting their sleep just long enough to devour eight or ten pounds of lasagna a week. They lumber out in the spring like a couple of water buffalo. A bird could land on one of their backs, and they would be too stuffed to care. My cats make Garfield look anorexic. Nevertheless, curled up on a braided rug, their legs wrapped around each other, their beautiful feline presence enhances the warmth of the room.

Sometimes it takes a deep snow and a howling wind to make us appreciate the cozy comfort of our shelter. When the weather is fine, home is a stopping-off place where we have an occasional meal or change our clothes for the next event, but a

Winding Roads

winter storm echoes the existence of a more primitive past. We are isolated from our neighbor and our customary pleasures. We are left to our own resources and must create our own entertainment.

    I turn off the television and the computer in favor of knitting or reading a book. I become a pilgrim searching for an earlier day when life was composed of simpler pleasures. As darkness falls and the outside cold seeps through the walls, I realize that this is a night to savor and hold forever.

About the Author

Helen Powers is an award-winning author and playwright who has been writing a weekly newspaper column called *Winding Roads* for the *New Fairfield Citizen News* for the past ten years. For eighteen years the writer lectured at women's clubs throughout the East, her subject being *How to Live Like a Super Star*, based on what she learned working in theater for seven years with super stars such as Marlene Dietrich, Jack Benny, Jerry Lewis and Guy Lombardo.

Ms Powers is the widow of a patent attorney with two grown sons, two grandchildren, a dog named Phoebe and a cat named Buck. Born in Alton, Illinois, and raised in St. Louis, she has lived in Connecticut for the past thirty years.